Non-League Football Supporters' Guide & Yearbook 2019

EDITOR
Steve Askew

Twenty-seventh Edition

For details of our range of over 2,300 books and around 300 DVDs, visit our web site or contact us using the information shown below.

British Library Cataloguing in Publication Data
A catalogue record for this book is available from the British Library

ISBN: 978-1-86223-380-5

Manufactured in the UK by Short Run Press Limited.

FOREWORD

Our thanks go to the numerous club officials who have aided us in the compilation of information contained in this guide as well as Michael Robinson (page layouts), Bob Budd (cover artwork) and Tony Brown (Cup Statistics – www.soccerdata.com).

Any readers who have up-to-date ground photographs which they would like us to consider for use in a future edition of this guide are requested to contact us at our address which is shown on the facing page.

The fixtures listed later in this book were released just a short time before we went to print and, as such, some of the dates shown may be subject to change. We therefore suggest that readers treat these fixtures as a rough guide and check dates carefully before attending matches.

We would like to wish our readers a safe and happy spectating season.

Steve Askew
EDITOR

CONTENTS

THE VANARAMA NATIONAL LEAGUE

Address   4th Floor, 20 Waterloo Street, Birmingham   B2 5TB

Phone (0121) 643-3143

Web site   www.footballconference.co.uk

Clubs for the 2018/2019 Season

AFC FYLDE

Photo courtesy of John Mills @ Altius Photography

Founded: 1988
Former Names: Formed by the amalgamation of Wesham FC and Kirkham Town FC in 1988
Nickname: 'The Coasters'
Ground: Mill Farm, Coronation Way, Wesham, Preston   PR4 3JZ
Record Attendance: 3,858 (26th December 2016)

Colours: White shirts and shorts
Telephone Nº: (01772) 682593
Fax Number: (01772) 685893
Ground Capacity: 6,000
Seating Capacity: 2,000
Pitch Size: 110 × 72 yards
Web Site: www.afcfylde.co.uk
E-mail: info@afcfylde.co.uk

GENERAL INFORMATION

Car Parking: A limited number of spaces are available at the ground and there is an overflow parking facility nearby.
Coach Parking: At the ground
Nearest Railway Station: Kirkham & Wesham (1 mile)
Club Shop: At the ground
Opening Times: Monday to Saturday 10.00am to 5.00pm. Tuesday Matchdays 10.00am to 10.00pm and Saturday Matchdays 9.00am to 6.00pm
Telephone Nº: (01772) 682593 (Phone orders accepted)

GROUND INFORMATION

Away Supporters' Entrances & Sections:
South Terrace standing and Seating in Block A.

ADMISSION INFO (2018/2019 PRICES)

Adult Standing: £14.00
Adult Seating: £18.00
Under-16s Standing: £5.00 (Free of charge for members)
Under-16s Seating: £10.00 (Free of charge for members)
Programme Price: £2.00

DISABLED INFORMATION

Wheelchairs: Accommodated
Helpers: Admitted
Prices: Normal prices apply for the disabled. One helper is admitted free of charge with each paying disabled fan.
Disabled Toilets: Available
Contact: (01772) 682593   (Bookings are necessary)

Travelling Supporters' Information:
Routes: The Mill Farm Sports Village is situated by the side of the A585, just to the north of Wesham and less than a mile to the south of Junction 3 of the M55.

ALDERSHOT TOWN FC

Founded: 2013 (as a new company)
Former Names: Aldershot Town FC
Nickname: 'Shots'
Ground: Ebb Stadium, High Street, Aldershot, GU11 1TW
Record Attendance: 7,500 (18th November 2000)
Pitch Size: 117 × 76 yards

Colours: Red shirts with Blue shorts
Telephone Nº: (01252) 320211
Club Secretary: (01252) 320211– Bob Green
Ground Capacity: 7,100
Seating Capacity: 2,042
Web site: www.theshots.co.uk
E-mail: admin@theshots.co.uk

GENERAL INFORMATION

Car Parking: Parsons Barracks Car Park is adjacent
Coach Parking: Contact the club for information
Nearest Railway Station: Aldershot (5 mins. walk)
Nearest Bus Station: Aldershot (5 minutes walk)
Club Shop: At the ground
Opening Times: Saturday matchdays 10.00am to 2.45pm and 9.30am to 7.30pm on Tuesday matchdays.
Telephone Nº: (01252) 320211

GROUND INFORMATION

Away Supporters' Entrances & Sections:
Accommodation in the East Bank Terrace, Bill Warren section (South Stand) – Redan Hill Turnstiles Nº 11 and 12.

ADMISSION INFO (2018/2019 PRICES)

Adult Standing: £14.00   **Adult Seating**: £20.00
Ages 11 to 18 Standing: £5.00
Ages 11 to 18 Seating: £7.00
Note: Under-11s are admitted free with paying adults – a maximum of 2 children per adult.
Concessionary Standing: £14.00
Concessionary Seating: £16.00
Note: Military personnel are charged Concessionary prices
Programme Price: £3.00

DISABLED INFORMATION

Wheelchairs: Accommodated in both the North Stand and the away section
Helpers: Admitted
Prices: Normal prices for the disabled, free for helpers
Disabled Toilets: Available
Contact: (01252) 320211   (Bookings are required)

Travelling Supporters' Information:
Routes: From the M3: Exit at Junction 4 and follow signs for Aldershot (A331). Leave the A331 at the A323 exit (Ash Road) and continue along into the High Street. The ground is just past the Railway Bridge on the right; From the A31: Continue along the A31 to the junction with the A331, then as above; From the A325 (Farnborough Road): Follow signs to the A323 then turn left into Wellington Avenue. The ground is just off the 2nd roundabout on the left – the floodlights are clearly visible.

BARNET FC

Founded: 1888
Former Names: Barnet Alston FC
Nickname: 'The Bees'
Ground: The Hive, Camrose Avenue, Edgware, HA8 6AG
Record Attendance: 5,539 (5th May 2018)
Pitch Size: 112 × 73 yards

Colours: Shirts and shorts are Black and Amber
Telephone Nº: (020) 8381-3800
Ticket Office: (020) 8381-3800
Ground Capacity: 6,205
Seating Capacity: 5,334
Web site: www.barnetfc.com
E-mail: justtellus@barnetfc.com

GENERAL INFORMATION

Car Parking: 350 spaces available at the ground
Coach Parking: Available at the ground
Nearest Railway Station: Harrow & Wealdstone (2½ miles)
Nearest Tube Station: Canons Park (5 minutes walk)
Club Shop: At the ground
Opening Times: Daily from 6.00am to midnight – the shop is open throughout The Hive opening hours.
Telephone Nº: (020) 8381-3800

GROUND INFORMATION

Away Supporters' Entrances & Sections:
North Terrace and North West corner

ADMISSION INFO (2018/2019 PRICES)

Adult Standing: £19.00
Adult Seating: £19.00 – £25.00
Concessionary Seating: £10.00 – £14.00
Under-17s Standing/Seating: £5.00
Away Supporter Seating: £23.00
Programme Price: £3.00

FANS WITH DISABILITIES INFORMATION

Wheelchairs: 43 covered spaces in total for Home and Away fans in the East and West Stands
Helpers: One helper admitted per wheelchair
Prices: Normal prices for fans with disabilities. Helpers free
Disabled Toilets: Available
Contact: (020) 8381-3800 (Bookings are advisable)

Travelling Supporters' Information:
Routes: Exit the M1 at Junction 4 and take the Edgware Way/Watford Bypass (A41). Take the 3rd exit at the roundabout onto the A410 then the first exit at the next roundabout along the A5 (Stonegrove), continuing for approximately 1½ miles. Turn right into Camrose Avenue and The Hive is approximately two-thirds of a mile along this road.

BARROW AFC

Founded: 1901
Former Names: None
Nickname: 'Bluebirds'
Ground: Furness Building Society Stadium,
Barrow-in-Furness, Cumbria   LA14 5UW
Record Attendance: 16,874 (1954)
Pitch Size: 110 × 75 yards

Colours: White shirts with Blue shorts
Telephone N°: (01229) 666061
Ground Capacity: 5,045
Seating Capacity: 1,000
Web site: www.barrowafc.com
E-mail: office@barrowafc.com

GENERAL INFORMATION

Car Parking: Street Parking, Popular Side Car Park and
Soccer Bar Car Park
Coach Parking: Adjacent to the ground
Nearest Railway Station: Barrow Central (½ mile)
Nearest Bus Station: ½ mile
Club Shop: At the ground
Opening Times: Monday to Friday 9.00am to 4.00pm and
Saturday Home Matchdays 12.00pm to 2.55pm.
Telephone N°: (01229) 666061

GROUND INFORMATION

Away Supporters' Entrances & Sections:
West Terrace (not covered)

ADMISSION INFO (2018/2019 PRICES)

Adult Standing: £15.00
Adult Seating: £18.00
Concessionary Standing: £12.00
Concessionary Seating: £14.00
Young Adult (Ages 18-22) Standing: £8.00
Young Adult (Ages 18-22) Seating: £10.00
Under-18s Standing: £5.00
Under-18s Seating: £8.00
Note: Under-12s are admitted free with a paying adult

DISABLED INFORMATION

Wheelchairs: 6 spaces available in the Disabled Area
Helpers: Admitted
Prices: Normal prices apply
Disabled Toilets: Available
Contact: (01229) 666061   (Bookings are not necessary)

Travelling Supporters' Information:
Routes: Exit the M6 at Junction 36 and take the A590 through Ulverston. Using the bypass, follow signs for Barrow. After
approximately 5 miles, turn left into Wilkie Road and the ground is on the right.

BOREHAM WOOD FC

Founded: 1948
Former Names: Boreham Rovers FC and Royal Retournez FC
Nickname: 'The Wood'
Ground: Meadow Park, Broughinge Road, Borehamwood, Hertfordshire   WD6 5AL
Record Attendance: 4,030 (2002)
Pitch Size: 112 × 72 yards

Colours: White shirts with Black shorts
Telephone Nº: (0208) 953-5097
Fax Number: (0208) 207-7982
Ground Capacity: 4,500
Seating Capacity: 1,700
Web site: www.borehamwoodfootballclub.co.uk

GENERAL INFORMATION

Car Parking: At the ground or in Brook Road car park
Coach Parking: At the ground
Nearest Railway Station: Elstree & Borehamwood (1 mile)
Nearest Bus Station: Barnet
Club Shop: At the ground
Opening Times: 9.00am to 10.00pm Monday to Thursday; 9.00am to 6.00pm at weekends
Telephone Nº: (0208) 953-5097

GROUND INFORMATION

Away Supporters' Entrances & Sections:
No usual segregation

ADMISSION INFO (2018/2019 PRICES)

Adult Standing: £18.00
Adult Seating: £18.00
Under-16s Standing/Seating: £8.50
Under-12s Standing/Seating: £4.00
Senior Citizen Standing/Seating: £13.00

DISABLED INFORMATION

Wheelchairs: Accommodated
Helpers: Admitted
Prices: Normal prices are charged for the disabled. Helpers are admitted free of charge.
Disabled Toilets: Available
Contact: (0208) 953-5097   (Bookings are not necessary)

Travelling Supporters' Information:
Routes: Exit the M25 at Junction 23 and take the A1 South. After 2 miles, take the Borehamwood exit onto the dual carriageway and go over the flyover following signs for Borehamwood for 1 mile. Turn right at the Studio roundabout into Brook Road, then next right into Broughinge Road for the ground.

BRAINTREE TOWN FC

Founded: 1898
Former Names: Manor Works FC, Crittall Athletic FC, Braintree & Crittall Athletic FC and Braintree FC
Nickname: 'The Iron'
Ground: The Ironmongery Direct Stadium, Clockhouse Way, Braintree, Essex CM7 3DE
Record Attendance: 4,000 (May 1952)
Pitch Size: 110 × 70 yards

Ground Capacity: 4,222
Seating Capacity: 553
Colours: Orange shirts and socks with Blue shorts
Telephone Nº: (01376) 345617
Fax Number: (01376) 330976
Web site: www.braintreetownfc.org.uk
E-mail: braintreetfc@aol.com

GENERAL INFORMATION
Car Parking: At the ground
Coach Parking: At the ground
Nearest Railway Station: Braintree (1 mile)
Nearest Bus Station: Braintree
Club Shop: At the ground
Opening Times: Matchdays only
Telephone Nº: (01376) 345617

GROUND INFORMATION
Away Supporters' Entrances & Sections: Gates 7-8

ADMISSION INFO (2018/2019 PRICES)
Adult Standing: £15.00 – £19.00
Adult Seating: £15.00 – £19.00
Concessionary Standing: £12.00
Concessionary Seating: £12.00
Under-18s Standing: £5.00

DISABLED INFORMATION
Wheelchairs: Accommodated – 6 spaces available in the Main Stand
Helpers: Admitted
Prices: Normal prices apply for fans with disabilities. Helpers are admitted free of charge
Disabled Toilets: Available
Contact: (01376) 345617

Travelling Supporters' Information:
Routes: Exit the A120 Braintree Bypass at the McDonald's roundabout and follow Cressing Road northwards. The floodlights at the ground are visible on the left ½ mile into town. Turn left into Clockhouse Way then left again for the ground.

BROMLEY FC

Founded: 1892
Former Names: None
Nickname: 'Lillywhites'
Ground: The Stadium, Hayes Lane, Bromley, Kent, BR2 9EF
Record Attendance: 10,798 (24th September 1949)
Pitch Size: 112 × 72 yards

Colours: White shirts with Black shorts
Telephone Nº: (020) 8460-5291
Fax Number: (020) 8313-3992
Ground Capacity: 5,000
Seating Capacity: 1,300
Web site: www.bromleyfc.tv
E-mail: info@bromleyfc.co.uk

GENERAL INFORMATION

Car Parking: 300 spaces available at the ground
Coach Parking: At the ground
Nearest Railway Station: Bromley South (1 mile)
Nearest Bus Station: High Street, Bromley
Club Shop: At the ground
Opening Times: Matchdays only
Telephone Nº: (020) 8460-5291

GROUND INFORMATION

Away Supporters' Entrances & Sections:
No usual segregation

ADMISSION INFO (2018/2019 PRICES)

Adult Standing/Seating: £15.00 (£18.00)
Concessionary Standing/Seating: £10.00 (£12.00)
Under-16s/Student Standing/Seating: £5.00 (£10.00)
Note: Prices shown are for tickets purchased in advance. Tickets purchased just before the game are more expensive (prices shown above in brackets). Discounted prices are available on the matchday for online bookings before 1.30pm or 6.30pm for day and night matches respectively. Under-16s are admitted free of charge with a paying adult for advance purchases up to 1 hour before kick-off.
A special £10.00 discounted price is available for Season Ticket holders of Premiership and Football League clubs.

DISABLED INFORMATION

Wheelchairs: Accommodated
Helpers: Admitted
Prices: Please phone the club for information
Disabled Toilets: Available
Contact: (0181) 460-5291 (Bookings are necessary)

Travelling Supporters' Information:
Routes: Exit the M25 at Junction 4 and follow the A21 for Bromley and London for approximately 4 miles before forking left onto the A232 signposted for Croydon/Sutton. At the second set of traffic lights turn right into Baston Road (B265) and follow for approximately 2 miles as it becomes Hayes Street and then Hayes Lane. The ground is on the right just after a mini-roundabout.

CHESTERFIELD FC

Founded: 1866
Former Names: Chesterfield Municipal FC,
Chesterfield Town FC
Nickname: 'Spireites' 'Blues'
Ground: Proact Stadium , 1866 Sheffield Road,
Whittington Moor, Chesterfield   S41 8NZ
Ground Capacity: 10,300 (All seats)

Record Attendance: 30,968 (Saltergate – 7/4/1939)
Pitch Size: 112 × 71 yards
Colours: Blue shirts with White shorts
Telephone Nº: (01246) 269300
Fax Number: (01246) 556799
Web Site: www.chesterfield-fc.co.uk

GENERAL INFORMATION

Car Parking: Various Car Parks available nearby
Coach Parking: At the ground
Nearest Railway Station: Chesterfield (1¼ miles)
Nearest Bus Station: Chesterfield
Club Shop: At the ground
Opening Times: Monday to Friday 9.00am to 5.00pm.
Saturday 10.00am to 3.00pm on matchdays only
Telephone Nº: (01246) 209765

GROUND INFORMATION

Away Supporters' Entrances & Sections:
North (Rubicon Stand) Turnstiles

ADMISSION INFO (2018/2019 PRICES)

Adult Seating: £16.00 – £20.00
Ages 17 to 21 Seating: £8.00 – £13.00
Juvenile (Under-17s) Seating: £6.00 – £9.00
(£4.00 in the family stand)
Concessionary Seating: £12.00 – £16.00
Under-7s Seating: £2.00 in the Family Stand
Note: Prices may vary depending on the category of the game
Programme Price: £3.00

FANS WITH DISABILITIES INFORMATION

Wheelchairs: Up to 100 spaces available around the ground
Note: Lifts are available in the East and West stands
Helpers: One helper admitted per fan with disabilities
Prices: Concessionary prices for fans with disabilities.
One helper admitted free of charge with each fan.
Disabled Toilets: Available in all stands
Contact: (01246) 269300   (Bookings are advised)

Travelling Supporters' Information:
Routes: From the South: Exit the M1 at Junction 29 and follow the A617 for Chesterfield. At the roundabout, take the 4th exit and head north on the A61 Sheffield Road and the stadium is located in the Whittington Moor district next to the junction with the A619; From the East: Take the A619 to Chesterfield and the ground is situated next to the Tesco supermarket at the junction with the A61; From the North: Exit the M1 at Junction 30 and take the A619 to Chesterfield. Then as above.

DAGENHAM & REDBRIDGE FC

Founded: 1992   (**Entered League**: 2007)
Former Names: Formed by the merger of
Dagenham FC and Redbridge Forest FC
Nickname: 'The Daggers'
Ground: Chigwell Construction Stadium,
Victoria Road, Dagenham   RM10 7XL
Record Attendance: 5,949 (vs Ipswich Town in 2002)
Pitch Size: 110 × 70 yards

Colours: Red and Blue striped shirts with Blue shorts
Telephone N°: (020) 8592-1549
Office Phone N°: (020) 8592-7194
Secretary's Phone N°: (020) 8592-1549
Fax Number: (020) 8593-7227
Ground Capacity: 6,078 **Seating Capacity**: 2,233
Web site: www.daggers.co.uk
E-mail: info@daggers.co.uk

GENERAL INFORMATION

Car Parking: Street parking only
Coach Parking: Street parking only
Nearest Railway Station: Dagenham East (5 mins. walk)
Nearest Bus Station: Romford
Club Shop: At the ground
Opening Times: Monday & Tuesday 12.00pm – 4.00pm;
Thursday 12.00pm – 8.00pm; Friday 12.00pm – 6.00pm;
Saturday matchdays 1.00pm – 3.00pm.
Closed on Wednesdays, Sundays and non-match Saturdays
Telephone N°: (020) 8592-7194

GROUND INFORMATION

Away Supporters' Entrances & Sections:
Pondfield Road entrances for the A13 Steel Stand

ADMISSION INFO (2018/2019 PRICES)

Adult Standing: £15.00
Adult Seating: £15.00 – £21.00
Concessionary Standing: £10.00
Concessionary Seating: £10.00 – £15.00
Under-16s Standing: £8.00 (Under-10s free of charge)
Under-16s Seating: £8.00 – £12.00
Under-10s Seating: £2.00 (Free in the Family Stand)

DISABLED INFORMATION

Wheelchairs: Accommodated in front of the new Stand
and the Barking College Stand
Helpers: Admitted
Prices: £15.00 for the disabled. Free of charge for Helpers
Disabled Toilets: Available at the East and West ends of the
ground and also in the Clubhouse
Contact: (020) 8592-7194 (Bookings are necessary)

Travelling Supporters' Information:
Routes: From the North & West: Take the M11 to its end and join the A406 South. At the large roundabout take the slip road on the left signposted A13 to Dagenham. As you approach Dagenham, stay in the left lane and follow signs for A1306 signposted Dagenham East. Turn left onto the A1112 at the 5th set of traffic lights by the McDonalds. Proceed along Ballards Road to The Bull roundabout and bear left. Victoria Road is 450 yards on the left after passing Dagenham East tube station; From the South & East: Follow signs for the A13 to Dagenham. Take the next slip road off signposted Elm Park & Dagenham East then turn right at the roundabout. Go straight on at the next roundabout and turn left onto A1306. After ½ mile you will see a McDonalds on the right. Get into the right hand filter lane and turn right onto A1112. Then as from the North & West.   **SatNav**: RM10 7XL

DOVER ATHLETIC FC

Founded: 1983
Former Names: None
Nickname: 'The Whites'
Ground: Crabble Athletic Ground, Lewisham Road, River, Dover   CT17 0JB
Record Attendance: 7,000 (vs Folkestone in 1951)
Pitch Size: 111 × 73 yards

Colours: White shirts with Black shorts
Telephone Nº: (01304) 822373
Fax Number: (01304) 821383
Ground Capacity: 5,745
Seating Capacity: 1,500
Web site: www.doverathletic.com
E-mail: enquiries@doverathletic.com

GENERAL INFORMATION

Car Parking: Street parking
Coach Parking: Street parking
Nearest Railway Station: Kearsney (1 mile)
Nearest Bus Station: Pencester Road, Dover (1½ miles)
Club Shop: At the ground
Opening Times: Saturdays 9.00am to 12.00pm
Telephone Nº: (01304) 822373

GROUND INFORMATION

Away Supporters' Entrances & Sections:
Segregation only used when required

ADMISSION INFO (2018/2019 PRICES)

Adult Standing: £17.00
Adult Seating: £18.50
Senior Citizen Standing: £14.00
Senior Citizen Seating: £15.00
Under-18s Standing: £8.00
Under-18s Seating: £9.00
Under-11s Standing/Seating: Free of charge

DISABLED INFORMATION

Wheelchairs: Approximately 6 spaces are available in the Family Stand
Helpers: Please phone the club for information
Prices: Please phone the club for information
Disabled Toilets: Three available
Contact: –   (Bookings are not necessary)

Travelling Supporters' Information:
Routes: Take the A2 to the Whitfield roundabout and take the 4th exit. Travel down the hill to the mini-roundabout then turn left and follow the road for 1 mile to the traffic lights on the hill. Turn sharp right and pass under the railway bridge – the ground is on the left after 300 yards.

EASTLEIGH FC

Founded: 1946
Former Names: Swaythling Athletic FC and Swaythling FC
Nickname: 'The Spitfires'
Ground: The Silverlake Stadium, Stoneham Lane, Eastleigh   SO50 9HT
Record Attendance: 5,025 (2016)
Pitch Size: 112 × 74 yards

Colours: Blue shirts with White shorts
Telephone Nº: (023) 8061-3361
Fax Number: (023) 8061-2379
Ground Capacity: 5,192
Seating Capacity: 3,210
Web site: www.eastleighfc.com
e-mail: admin@eastleighfc.com

GENERAL INFORMATION

Car Parking: Spaces for 450 cars available (hard standing)
Coach Parking: At the ground
Nearest Railway Station: Southampton Parkway (¾ mile)
Nearest Bus Station: Eastleigh (2 miles)
Club Shop: At the ground
Opening Times: Matchdays and during functions only

GROUND INFORMATION

Away Supporters' Entrances & Sections:
South Stand, entrance via Gates 10 and 11

ADMISSION INFO (2018/2019 PRICES)

Adult Standing: £15.00   **Adult Seating**: £18.00
Concessionary Standing: £10.00
Concessionary Seating: £12.00
Under-18s Standing/Seating: £4.00 or £7.50
Under-7s Standing: Free of charge
Under-7s Seating: £3.00
Note: Discounted prices are available for advance purchases

DISABLED INFORMATION

Wheelchairs: Over 20 spaces available.
Helpers: Admitted
Prices: Normal prices for the disabled. Helpers free of charge
Disabled Toilets: Available
Contact: (023) 8061-3361   (Bookings are not necessary)

Travelling Supporters' Information:
Routes: Exit the M27 at Junction 5 (signposted for Southampton Airport) and take the A335 (Stoneham Way) towards Southampton. After ½ mile, turn right at the traffic lights into Bassett Green Road. Turn right at the next set of traffic lights into Stoneham Lane and the ground is on the right after ¾ mile.

EBBSFLEET UNITED FC

Founded: 1946
Former Names: Gravesend & Northfleet United FC, Gravesend United FC and Northfleet United FC
Nickname: 'The Fleet'
Ground: The Kuflink Stadium, Stonebridge Road, Northfleet, Gravesend, Kent DA11 9GN
Record Attendance: 12,036 (vs Sunderland 1963)
Pitch Size: 112 × 72 yards

Colours: Reds shirts with White shorts
Telephone Nº: (01474) 533796
Fax Number: (01474) 324754
Ground Capacity: 4,769
Seating Capacity: 2,179
Web site: www.ebbsfleetunited.co.uk
E-mail: info@eufc.co.uk

GENERAL INFORMATION

Car Parking: Ebbsfleet International Car Park C (when available) and also street parking
Coach Parking: At the ground
Nearest Railway Station: Northfleet (5 minutes walk)
Nearest Bus Station: Bus Stop outside the ground
Club Shop: At the ground
Opening Times: Weekdays 9.00am to 5.00pm
Telephone Nº: (01474) 533796

GROUND INFORMATION

Away Supporters' Entrances & Sections:
Only certain games are segregated, when the Swanscombe End turnstiles are allocated to away supporters.
Please contact the club for further details

ADMISSION INFO (2018/2019 PRICES)

Adult Standing: £15.00
Adult Seating: £15.00
Concessionary Standing: £12.00
Concessionary Seating: £12.00
Under-16s Standing/Seating: £7.00
Under-12s Standing/Seating: Free of charge when accompanied by a paying adult (maximum of 2 per adult).

DISABLED INFORMATION

Wheelchairs: 6 spaces are available in the Disabled Area in front of the Main Stand
Helpers: Admitted free of charge
Prices: Normal prices apply for disabled fans
Disabled Toilets: Available in the Main Stand
Contact: (01474) 533796 (Bookings are necessary)

Travelling Supporters' Information:
Routes: Take the A2 to the Northfleet/Southfleet exit and follow signs for Northfleet (B262). Go straight on at the first roundabout then take the 2nd exit at the 2nd roundabout into Thames Way and follow the football signs for the ground.

FC HALIFAX TOWN

Founded: 1911 (Re-formed 2008)
Former Names: Halifax Town FC
Nickname: 'The Shaymen'
Ground: The MBi Shay Stadium, Shay Syke, Halifax, HX1 2YT
Ground Capacity: 10,568
Seating Capacity: 5,285

Record Attendance: 8,042 (vs Bradford City, 2014)
Pitch Size: 112 × 73 yards
Colours: Blue shirts and shorts
Telephone Nº: (01422) 341222
Fax Number: (01422) 349487
Web Site: www.fchalifaxtown.co.uk

GENERAL INFORMATION

Car Parking: Adjacent to the East Stand and also Shaw Hill Car Park (Nearby)
Coach Parking: By arrangement with the Club Secretary
Nearest Railway Station: Halifax (10 minutes walk)
Nearest Bus Station: Halifax (15 minutes walk)
Club Shop: At the ground in the East Stand
Opening Times: Please phone for details
Telephone Nº: (01422) 341222

GROUND INFORMATION

Away Supporters' Entrances & Sections:
Skircoat Stand (Seating only)

ADMISSION INFO (2018/2019 PRICES)

Adult Standing/Seating: £20.00
Senior Citizen Standing/Seating: £17.00
Under-12s Standing/Seating: £5.00
Under-7s Standing/Seating: £3.00

DISABLED INFORMATION

Wheelchairs: 33 spaces available in total in disabled sections in the East Stand and South Stand
Helpers: One admitted free with each paying disabled fan
Prices: Free of charge for the disabled and helpers
Disabled Toilets: Available in the East and South Stands
Contact: (01422) 341222 (Bookings are not necessary)

Travelling Supporters' Information:
Routes: From the North: Take the A629 to Halifax Town Centre. Take the 2nd exit at the roundabout into Broad Street and follow signs for Huddersfield (A629) into Skircoat Road; From the South, East and West: Exit the M62 at Junction 24 and follow Halifax (A629) signs for the Town Centre into Skircoat Road then Shaw Hill for ground. **SatNav**: Use HX1 2YS for the ground.

GATESHEAD FC

Founded: 1930 (Reformed in 1977)
Former Names: Gateshead United FC
Nickname: 'Tynesiders'
Ground: International Stadium, Neilson Road, Gateshead   NE10 0EF
Record Attendance: 11,750 (vs Newcastle Utd, 1995)
Pitch Size: 110 × 70 yards

Colours: White shirts with Black shorts
Telephone Nº: (0191) 478-3883
Fax Number: (0191) 440-0404
Ground Capacity: 11,750
Seating Capacity: 11,750
Web site: www.gateshead-fc.com
E-mail: info@gateshead-fc.com

GENERAL INFORMATION
Car Parking: At the stadium
Coach Parking: At the stadium
Nearest Railway Station: Gateshead Stadium Metro (½ mile); Newcastle (British Rail) 1½ miles
Nearest Bus Station: Newcastle Coach Station, St. James' Boulevard, Newcastle-upon-Tyne, NE1 4BW   (2½ miles)
Club Shop: At the stadium
Opening Times: Matchdays only
Telephone Nº: (0191) 478-3883

GROUND INFORMATION
Away Supporters' Entrances & Sections:
Tyne & Wear County Stand North End or the East Stand

ADMISSION INFO (2018/2019 PRICES)
Adult Seating: £15.00
Senior Citizen/Concessionary Seating: £8.00
Under-16s/Student Seating: £3.00
Family Ticket: £25.00 (2 Adults + 2 Children)
Note: Under-12s are admitted free of charge when accompanied by a paying adult.

DISABLED INFORMATION
Wheelchairs: 5 spaces available each for home and away fans by the trackside – Level access with automatic doors
Helpers: Admitted
Prices: Normal prices for the disabled. Helpers are admitted free of charge.
Disabled Toilets: Available in the Reception Area and on the 1st floor concourse – accessible by lift.
Contact: (0191) 478-3883   (Bookings are necessary)

Travelling Supporters' Information:
Routes: From the South: Take the A1(M) to Washington Services and fork right onto the A194(M) signposted Tyne Tunnel. At the next roundabout, turn left onto the A184 signposted for Gateshead. The Stadium is on the right after 3 miles.

HARROGATE TOWN AFC

Founded: 1919
Former Names: Harrogate FC and Harrogate Hotspurs FC
Nickname: 'Town'
Ground: CNG Stadium, Wetherby Road, Harrogate, HG2 7SA
Record Attendance: 15,000 (vs Sheffield Utd, 1920)
Pitch Size: 107 × 72 yards

Colours: Yellow and Black striped shirts, Black shorts
Telephone Nº: (01423) 210600
Ground Capacity: 3,800
Seating Capacity: 502
Web site: www.harrogatetownafc.com
E-mail: enquiries@harrogatetownafc.com

GENERAL INFORMATION

Car Parking: Hospital Car Park adjacent
Coach Parking: At the ground
Nearest Railway Station: Harrogate (¾ mile)
Nearest Bus Station: Harrogate
Club Shop: At the ground
Opening Times: Monday to Friday 9.00am to 3.00pm and also on Matchdays
Telephone Nº: (01423) 210600

GROUND INFORMATION

Away Supporters' Entrances & Sections:
No usual segregation

ADMISSION INFO (2018/2019 PRICES)

Adult Standing: £14.00 – £16.00
Adult Seating: £15.00 – £17.00
Concessionary/Ages 17 to 21 Standing: £10.00 – £12.00
Concessionary/Ages 17 to 21 Seating: £11.00 – £13.00
Under-16s Standing: £5.00 – £6.00
Under-16s Seating: £6.00 – £7.00
Note: Tickets are cheaper when purchased in advance online.

DISABLED INFORMATION

Wheelchairs: Accommodated at the front of the Main Stand
Helpers: One helper admitted for each disabled fan
Prices: Free of charge for each disabled fan and helper
Disabled Toilets: Available
Contact: (01423) 880675 (Bookings are necessary)

Travelling Supporters' Information:
Routes: From the South: Take the A61 from Leeds and turn right at the roundabout onto the ring road (signposted York). After about 1¼ miles turn left at the next roundabout onto A661 Wetherby Road. The ground is situated ¾ mile on the right; From the West: Take the A59 straight into Wetherby Road from Empress Roundabout and the ground is on the left; From the East & North: Exit the A1(M) at Junction 47, take the A59 to Harrogate then follow the Southern bypass to Wetherby Road for the A661 Roundabout. Turn right towards Harrogate Town Centre and the ground is on the right after ¾ mile.

HARTLEPOOL UNITED FC

Founded: 1908
Former Names: Hartlepools United FC (1908-68); Hartlepool FC (1968-77)
Nickname: 'The Pool' 'Pools'
Ground: Victoria Park, Clarence Road, Hartlepool, TS24 8BZ
Ground Capacity: 7,865 **Seating Capacity**: 4,249
Record Attendance: 17,426 (15th January 1957)

Pitch Size: 110 × 74 yards
Colours: Blue and White striped shirts with Blue shorts
Telephone Nº: (01429) 272584
Ticket Office: (01429) 272584 Extension 2
Ticket Office e-mail: tickets@hartlepoolunited.co.uk
Fax Number: (01429) 863007
Web Site: www.hartlepoolunited.co.uk
E-mail: enquiries@hartlepoolunited.co.uk

GENERAL INFORMATION

Car Parking: Limited space at the ground (£8.00 charge) and also street parking
Coach Parking: Church Street
Nearest Railway Station: Hartlepool Church Street (5 minutes walk)
Club Shop: At the ground
Opening Times: Please contact the club for details
Telephone Nº: (01429) 260491

GROUND INFORMATION

Away Supporters' Entrances & Sections:
Clarence Road turnstiles 1 & 2 for Smith & Graham Stand

ADMISSION INFO (2018/2019 PRICES)

Adult Standing: £18.00
Adult Seating: £20.00
Senior Citizen/Under-19s/Student Standing: £9.00
Senior Citizen/Under-19s/Student Seating: £10.00
Under-16s: Admitted for £5.00 with a paying adult
Programme Price: £3.00

DISABLED INFORMATION

Wheelchairs: 21 spaces for Home fans in disabled section, Cyril Knowles Stand, 10 spaces for Away fans in the Smith & Graham Stand.
Helpers: One helper admitted per wheelchair
Prices: £20.00 for the Disabled. Helpers free of charge
Disabled Toilets: Available in the Cyril Knowles Stand
Contact: (01429) 272584 (Bookings are advisable)

Travelling Supporters' Information: **Routes**: From the North: Take the A1/A19 to the A179 and follow Town Centre/ Marina signs. Turn right at the roundabout by the 'Historic Quayside' and cross over the Railway bridge. The ground is on the left; From the South & West: Take the A689 following Town Centre/Marina signs. Turn left at the roundabout by the 'Historic Quayside' and cross over the Railway bridge. The ground is on the left.

HAVANT & WATERLOOVILLE FC

Founded: 1998
Former Names: Formed by the amalgamation of Waterlooville FC and Havant Town FC
Nickname: 'The Hawks'
Ground: Westleigh Park, Martin Road, Havant, PO9 5TH
Record Attendance: 4,400 (2006/07)
Pitch Size: 112 × 76 yards

Colours: White shirts with Blue shorts
Telephone Nº: (023) 9278-7822 (Ground)
Fax Number: (023) 9226-2367
Ground Capacity: 5,300
Seating Capacity: 710
Web site: www.havantandwaterloovillefc.co.uk

GENERAL INFORMATION

Car Parking: Space for 300 cars at the ground
Coach Parking: At the ground
Nearest Railway Station: Havant (1 mile)
Nearest Bus Station: Town Centre (1½ miles)
Club Shop: At the ground
Opening Times: Matchdays only
Telephone Nº: 07768 271143

GROUND INFORMATION

Away Supporters' Entrances & Sections:
Martin Road End

ADMISSION INFO (2018/2019 PRICES)

Adult Standing: £16.00
Adult Seating: £16.00
Senior Citizen Standing/Seating: £12.00
Concessionary Standing/Seating: £12.00
Note: When accompanied by a paying adult, children under the age of 11 are admitted free of charge

DISABLED INFORMATION

Wheelchairs: 12 spaces available in the Main Stand
Helpers: Admitted
Prices: Normal prices for disabled fans. Free for helpers
Disabled Toilets: Two available
Contact: (023) 9226-7822 (Bookings are necessary)

Travelling Supporters' Information:
Routes: From London or the North take the A27 from Chichester and exit at the B2149 turn-off for Havant. Take the 2nd exit off the dual carriageway into Bartons Road and then the 1st right into Martin Road for the ground; From the West: Take the M27 then the A27 to the Petersfield exit. Then as above.

LEYTON ORIENT FC

Founded: 1881
Former Names: Glyn Cricket and Football Club
(1881-86); Eagle FC (1886-88); Clapton Orient FC
(1888-1946); Leyton Orient FC (1946-66); Orient FC
(1966-87)
Nickname: 'O's'
Ground: The Breyer Group Stadium, Brisbane Road,
Leyton, London   E10 5NF

Ground Capacity: 9,271 (all seats)
Record Attendance: 34,345 (21st January 1964)
Pitch Size: 110 × 76 yards
Telephone Nº: 0871 310-1881
Ticket Office: 0871 310-1883
Fax Number: 0871 310-1882
Web Site: www.leytonorient.com
E-mail: info@leytonorient.net

GENERAL INFORMATION
Car Parking: Street parking
Coach Parking: By Police direction
Nearest Railway Station: Leyton Midland Road (½ mile)
Nearest Tube Station: Leyton (Central)
Club Shop: At the ground
Opening Times: Weekdays and Home Matchdays 10.00am
to 3.00pm
Telephone Nº: 0871 310-1889

GROUND INFORMATION
Away Supporters' Entrances & Sections:
East Stand

ADMISSION INFO (2018/2019 PRICES)
Adult Seating: £18.00 – £30.00
Child Seating: £5.00 – (or £1.00 for Under-11s if booked in
advance in the North Family Stand only)
Concessionary Seating: £16.00 – £27.00
Note: Tickets are cheaper when purchased in advance
Programme Price: £3.00

DISABLED INFORMATION
Wheelchairs: Spaces are available in the North, East and
West Stands
Helpers: One helper admitted per disabled person
Prices: Free of charge for the disabled and helpers
Disabled Toilets: Available near disabled sections
Contact: 0871 310-1881   (Bookings are necessary)

Travelling Supporters' Information:
Routes: From the North & West: Take A406 North Circular, follow signs for Chelmsford to Edmonton. After 2½ miles take the
3rd exit at the roundabout towards Leyton (A112). Pass the railway station, turn right after ½ mile into Windsor Road and left
into Brisbane Road; From the East: Follow the A12 to London then the City for Leytonstone. Follow Hackney signs into Grove
Road, cross Main Road into Ruckholt Road then turn right into Leyton High Road, turn left after ¼ mile into Buckingham Road
and left into Brisbane Road; From the South: Take the A102M through the Blackwall Tunnel, follow signs for Newmarket (A102)
to join the A11 to Stratford, then follow signs for Stratford Station into Leyton Road to the railway station (then as from North).

MAIDENHEAD UNITED FC

Founded: 1870
Former Names: None
Nickname: 'Magpies'
Ground: York Road, Maidenhead, Berks. SL6 1SF
Record Attendance: 7,920 (1936)
Pitch Size: 110 × 75 yards

Colours: Black and White striped shirts, Black shorts
Telephone Nº: (01628) 636314 (Club)
Contact Number: (01628) 636314
Ground Capacity: 4,000
Seating Capacity: 550
Web: www.pitchero.com/clubs/maidenheadunited
E-mail: social@maidenheadunitedfc.org

GENERAL INFORMATION
Car Parking: Street parking
Coach Parking: Street parking
Nearest Railway Station: Maidenhead (¼ mile)
Nearest Bus Station: Maidenhead
Club Shop: At the ground
Opening Times: Matchdays only
Telephone Nº: (01628) 624739

GROUND INFORMATION
Away Supporters' Entrances & Sections:
No usual segregation

ADMISSION INFO (2018/2019 PRICES)
Adult Standing: £15.00
Adult Seating: £15.00
Concessionary Standing and Seating: £10.00
Under-16s Standing and Seating: £5.00
Note: Junior Magpies (Under-16s) are admitted free to
matches in the League.
Programme Price: £2.00

DISABLED INFORMATION
Wheelchairs: Accommodated
Helpers: Admitted
Prices: Normal prices for the disabled. Free for helpers
Disabled Toilets: Available
Contact: (01628) 636314   (Bookings are not necessary)

Travelling Supporters' Information:
Routes: Exit M4 at Junction 7 and take the A4 to Maidenhead. Cross the River Thames bridge and turn left at the 2nd roundabout
passing through the traffic lights. York Road is first right and the ground is approximately 300 yards along on the left.

MAIDSTONE UNITED FC |

Founded: 1992 (Reformed)
Former Names: Maidstone Invicta FC
Nickname: 'The Stones'
Ground: Gallagher Stadium, James Whatman Way, Maidstone ME14 1LQ
Record Attendance: 3,409 (29th April 2017)

Colours: Amber shirts with Black shorts
Telephone Nº: (01622) 753817
Ground Capacity: 4,191
Seating Capacity: 750
Web Site: www.maidstoneunited.co.uk

GENERAL INFORMATION

Car Parking: Various Pay & Display Car Parks available near the ground
Coach Parking: Maidstone coach park (1¼ miles) – please contact the club for further information
Nearest Railway Station: Maidstone East (¼ mile)
Club Shop: Available at the ground
Opening Times: Saturday Matchdays 12.30pm to 5.00pm; Tuesday Matchdays 6.15pm to 9.30pm.
Telephone Nº: (01622) 753817

GROUND INFORMATION

Away Supporters' Entrances & Sections:
No usual segregation – use the main turnstiles unless otherwise advertised.

ADMISSION INFO (2018/2019 PRICES)

Adult Standing: £15.00
Adult Seating: £18.00
Senior Citizen/Student Standing: £12.00
Senior Citizen/Student Seating: £15.00
Ages 11 to 16 Standing: £7.00
Ages 11 to 16 Seating: £10.00
Under-11s Standing: £2.00
Under-11s Seating: £5.00
Programme Price: £3.00

DISABLED INFORMATION

Wheelchairs: Accommodated
Helpers: Admitted
Prices: Normal prices apply for the disabled. Free for helpers
Disabled Toilets: Available
Contact: (01622) 753817 (Bookings are essential)

Travelling Supporters' Information:
Routes: Exit the M20 at Junction 6 or the M2 at Junction 3 and follow the A229 into Maidstone. After entering Maidstone, at the second roundabout (by the White Rabbit pub), take the third exit into James Whatman Way for the stadium. Please check the club web site for details of the nearest car parks.

SALFORD CITY FC

Founded: 1940
Former Names: Salford FC, Salford Amateurs FC plus a number of other early names
Nickname: 'The Ammies'
Ground: The Peninsula Stadium, Moor Lane, Salford, Manchester M7 3PZ
Record Attendance: 4,200 (vs 'Class of 92', 2017)

Colours: Red shirts with White shorts
Telephone Nº: (0161) 792-6287
Ground Capacity: 5,106
Seating Capacity: 2,246
Pitch Size: 110 × 70 yards
Web site: www.salfordcityfc.co.uk
E-mail: enquiries@salfordcityfc.co.uk

GENERAL INFORMATION
Car Parking: Street parking only
Coach Parking: At the ground
Nearest Railway Station: Clifton (2½ miles)
Club Shop: At the ground
Opening Times: Matchdays only
Telephone Nº: ()161) 792-6287

GROUND INFORMATION
Away Supporters' Entrances & Sections:
No usual segregation

ADMISSION INFO (2018/2019 PRICES)
Adult Standing: £10.00
Adult Seating: £10.00
Senior Citizen/Junior Standing: £5.00
Senior Citizen/Junior Seating: £5.00
Note: Under-5s are admitted free of charge when attending the game with a paying adult.

DISABLED INFORMATION
Wheelchairs: Accommodated
Helpers: Admitted
Prices: Normal prices are charged for fans with disabilities. Helpers are admitted free of charge
Disabled Toilets: Available in the club house
Contact: (0161) 792-6287 (Bookings are not necessary)

Travelling Supporters' Information:
Routes: Exit the M60 at Junction 17 and take the A56 Bury New Road towards Prestwich. Continue along, passing the A6044 (Hilton Lane) road then turn right along Moor Lane heading towards Kersal Moor and the Golf Course. The ground is on the left hand side of the road after a few hundred yards.

SOLIHULL MOORS FC

Photo courtesy of Jordan Martin Photography

Founded: 2007
Former Names: Formed by the merger of Solihull Borough FC and Moor Green FC in 2007
Nickname: 'The Moors'
Ground: The Autotmated Technology Group Stadium, Damson Parkway, Solihull B91 2PP
Record Attendance: 1,995 (vs Tranmere Rovers, 2016)
Pitch Size: 114 × 76 yards

Colours: Yellow and Blue hooped shirts, Blue shorts
Telephone Nº: (0121) 705-6770
Fax Number: (0121) 711-4045
Ground Capacity: 4,313
Seating Capacity: 1,000
Web site: www.solihullmoorsfc.co.uk
E-mail: info@solihullmoorsfc.co.uk

GENERAL INFORMATION

Car Parking: At the ground (£2.00 charge per car)
Coach Parking: At the ground
Nearest Railway Station: Birmingham International (2 miles)
Nearest Bus Station: Birmingham (5 miles)
Club Shop: At the ground
Opening Times: Matchdays only
Telephone Nº: (0121) 705-6770

GROUND INFORMATION

Away Supporters' Entrances & Sections:
No usual segregation

ADMISSION INFO (2018/2019 PRICES)

Adult Standing: £15.00
Adult Seating: £15.00
Senior Citizen/Junior Standing: £10.00
Senior Citizen/Junior Seating: £10.00
Note: Under-12s are admitted free of charge when accompanied by a paying adult

DISABLED INFORMATION

Wheelchairs: Spaces for 3 wheelchairs are available
Helpers: Admitted
Prices: Normal prices for fans with disabilities. Helpers free
Disabled Toilets: Available
Contact: (0121) 705-6770

Travelling Supporters' Information:
Routes: Exit the M42 at Junction 6 and take the A45 for 2 miles towards Birmingham. Turn left at the traffic lights near the Posthouse Hotel into Damson Parkway (signposted for Landrover/Damsonwood). Continue to the roundabout and come back along the other carriageway to the ground which is situated on the left after about 150 yards.

SUTTON UNITED FC

Founded: 1898
Former Names: Formed by the amalgamation of Sutton Guild Rovers FC and Sutton Association FC
Nickname: 'U's'
Ground: The Knights Community Stadium, Sutton Sports Ground, Gander Green Lane, Sutton SM1 2EY
Record Attendance: 14,000 (1970)

Colours: Amber shirts and shorts
Telephone Nº: (020) 8644-4440
Fax Number: (020) 8644-5120
Ground Capacity: 5,013
Seating Capacity: 765
Web site: www.suttonunited.net
E-mail: info@suttonunited.net

GENERAL INFORMATION

Car Parking: 150 spaces behind the Main Stand for permit holders only. Otherwise, street parking is usually possible
Coach Parking: Space for 1 coach in the car park
Nearest Railway Station: West Sutton (adjacent)
Club Shop: At the ground
Opening Times: Matchdays only
Telephone Nº: (020) 8644-4440

GROUND INFORMATION

Away Supporters' Entrances & Sections:
Collingwood Road entrances and accommodation

ADMISSION INFO (2018/2019 PRICES)

Adult Standing: £15.00
Adult Seating: £17.00
Child Standing: £3.00
Child Seating: £5.00
Senior Citizen Standing: £8.00
Senior Citizen Seating: £10.00

DISABLED INFORMATION

Wheelchairs: 8 spaces are available under cover accommodated on the track perimeter
Helpers: Admitted
Prices: Normal prices apply for the disabled. Free for helpers
Disabled Toilets: Available alongside the Standing Terrace
Contact: (020) 8644-4440   (Bookings are necessary)

Travelling Supporters' Information:
Routes: Exit the M25 at Junction 8 (Reigate Hill) and travel North on the A217 for approximately 8 miles. Cross the A232 then turn right at the traffic lights (past Goose & Granit Public House) into Gander Green Lane. The ground is 300 yards on the left; From London: Gander Green Lane crosses the Sutton bypass 1 mile south of Rose Hill Roundabout. Avoid Sutton Town Centre, especially on Saturdays.

WREXHAM AFC

Founded: 1864
Nickname: 'Red Dragons'
Ground: Racecourse Ground, Mold Road, Wrexham, North Wales LL11 2AH
Ground Capacity: 10,500 (all seats)
Record Attendance: 34,445 (26th January 1957)
Pitch Size: 111 × 68 yards

Colours: Red shirts with White shorts
Telephone Nº: (01978) 891864
Web Site: www.wrexhamafc.co.uk
E-mail: info@wrexhamfc.tv

GENERAL INFORMATION

Car Parking: Town car parks are nearby and also Glyndwr University (Mold End)
Coach Parking: By Police direction
Nearest Railway Station: Wrexham General (adjacent)
Nearest Bus Station: Wrexham (King Street)
Club Shop: At the ground under the bkoncepts Stand
Opening Times: Monday to Friday 10.00am to 5.00pm
Telephone Nº: (01978) 891864

GROUND INFORMATION

Away Supporters' Entrances & Sections:
Turnstiles 1-4 for the bkoncepts Stand

ADMISSION INFO (2018/2019 PRICES)

Adult Seating: £16.00 – £20.00
Concession Seniors/Under-21s Seating: £13.00–£15.00
Concession Over-80s/Under-18s Seating: £7.00 – £8.00
Under-11s Seating: £1.00 (with a paying adult)
Note: Discounts apply for advance purchases and Family tickets are also available

DISABLED INFORMATION

Wheelchairs: 35 spaces in the Mold Road Stand
Helpers: One helper admitted per wheelchair
Prices: Normal prices for the disabled. Free for helpers
Disabled Toilets: Available in the disabled section
Contact: (01978) 891864

Travelling Supporters' Information:
Routes: From the North and West: Take the A483 and the Wrexham bypass to the junction with the A541. Branch left at the roundabout and follow Wrexham signs into Mold Road; From the East: Take the A525 or A534 into Wrexham then follow the A541 signs into Mold Road; From the South: Take the the M6, then the M54 and follow the A5 and A483 to the Wrexham bypass and the junction with the A541. Branch right at the roundabout and follow signs for the Town Centre.

THE VANARAMA NATIONAL LEAGUE NORTH

Address

4th Floor, 20 Waterloo Street, Birmingham   B2 5TB

Phone (0121) 643-3143

Web site   www.footballconference.co.uk

Clubs for the 2018/2019 Season

AFC TELFORD UNITED

Founded: 2004
Former Names: Formed after Telford United FC went out of business. TUFC were previously known as Wellington Town FC
Nickname: 'The Bucks'
Ground: The New Bucks Head Stadium, Watling Street, Wellington, Telford TF1 2TU
Record Attendance: 13,000 (1935)

Pitch Size: 110 × 74 yards
Colours: White shirts and shorts
Telehone Nº: (01952) 640064
Fax Number: (01952) 640021
Ground Capacity: 6,300
Seating Capacity: 2,200
Web site: www.telfordunited.com
E-mail: office@telfordutd.co.uk

GENERAL INFORMATION

Car Parking: At the ground (£3.00 charge for cars)
Coach Parking: At the ground
Nearest Railway Station: Wellington
Nearest Bus Station: Wellington
Club Shop: At the ground
Opening Times: Saturday matchdays only from 1.30pm.
Telephone Nº: (01952) 640064

GROUND INFORMATION

Away Supporters' Entrances & Sections:
Frank Nagington Stand on the rare occasions when segregation is used

ADMISSION INFO (2017/2018 PRICES)

Adult Standing: £14.00
Adult Seating: £14.00
Under-16s Standing: £3.00
Under-16s Seating: £3.00
Under-20s Standing: £5.00
Under-20s Seating: £5.00
Concessionary Standing: £10.00
Concessionary Seating: £10.00
Please contact the club for 2018/2019 pricing information.

DISABLED INFORMATION

Wheelchairs: Accommodated at both ends of the ground
Helpers: Admitted
Prices: Normal prices apply
Disabled Toilets: Available by the Sir Stephen Roberts Stand
Contact: (01952) 640064   (Bookings are not necessary)

Travelling Supporters' Information:
Routes: Exit the M54 at Junction 6 and take the A518. Go straight on at the first roundabout, take the second exit at the next roundabout then turn left at the following roundabout. Follow the road round to the right then turn left into the car park.

ALFRETON TOWN FC

Founded: 1959
Former Names: None
Nickname: 'Reds'
Ground: The Impact Arena, North Street, Alfreton, Derbyshire DE55 7FZ
Record Attendance: 5,023 vs Matlock Town (1960)
Pitch Size: 110 × 75 yards

Colours: Red shirts and shorts
Telephone Nº: (01773) 830277
Ground Capacity: 3,600
Seating Capacity: 1,500
Web site: www.alfretontownfc.com
E-mail: enquiries@alfretontownfc.com

GENERAL INFORMATION

Car Parking: At the ground
Coach Parking: Available close to the ground
Nearest Railway Station: Alfreton (½ mile)
Nearest Bus Station: Alfreton (5 minutes walk)
Club Shop: At the ground
Opening Times: Weekdays 9.00am to 3.00pm
Telephone Nº: (01773) 830277

GROUND INFORMATION

Away Supporters' Entrances & Sections:
Segregation is usual so please check prior to the game

ADMISSION INFO (2018/2019 PRICES)

Adult Standing: £14.00
Adult Seating: £14.00
Senior Citizen Standing/Seating: £10.00
Ages 16 to 21 Standing/Seating: £10.00
Under-16s Standing: £2.00 (with a paying adult)
Under-16s Seating: £2.00 (with a paying adult)

DISABLED INFORMATION

Wheelchairs: Accommodated in dedicated areas of the ground
Helpers: Admitted
Prices: Normal prices for disabled fans. Free for helpers
Disabled Toilets: Available in Zones 3 and 8
Contact: (01773) 830277   (Bookings are not necessary)

Travelling Supporters' Information:
Routes: Exit the M1 at Junction 28 and take the A38 signposted for Derby. After 2 miles take the sliproad onto the B600 then go right at the main road towards the town centre. After ½ mile turn left down North Street and the ground is on the right after 200 yards.

ALTRINCHAM FC

Founded: 1891
Former Names: Broadheath FC
Nickname: 'The Robins'
Ground: The J. Davidson Stadium, Moss Lane, Altrincham   WA15 8AP
Record Attendance: 10,275 (February 1925)
Pitch Size: 110 × 72 yards
Web site: www.altrinchamfc.com

Colours: Red and White striped shirts, Black shorts
Telephone N°: (0161) 928-1045
Daytime Phone N°: (0161) 928-1045
Fax Number: (0161) 926-9934
Ground Capacity: 6,085
Seating Capacity: 1,154
E-mail: office@altrinchamfootballclub.co.uk

GENERAL INFORMATION
Car Parking: Limited street parking
Coach Parking: By Police Direction
Nearest Railway Station: Altrincham (15 minutes walk)
Nearest Bus Station: Altrincham
Club Shop: Inside the ground
Opening Times: Weekdays 9.00am to 5.00pm
Telephone N°: (0161) 928-1045

GROUND INFORMATION
Away Supporters' Entrances & Sections:
Hale End turnstiles and accommodation

ADMISSION INFO   (2018/2019 PRICES)
Adult Standing: £13.00
Adult Seating: £13.00
Concessionary Standing: £10.00
Concessionary Seating: £10.00
Ages 12-16 years Standing/Seating: £5.00
Under-12s Standing/Seating: £1.00

DISABLED INFORMATION
Wheelchairs: 3 spaces are available each for home and away fans adjacent to the Away dugout
Helpers: Admitted
Prices: £14.00 combined price for a disabled fan and helper
Disabled Toilets: Yes
Contact: (0161) 928-1045   (Bookings are necessary)

Travelling Supporters' Information:
Routes: Exit the M56 at either Junction 6 or 7 and follow the signs for Altrincham FC.

ASHTON UNITED FC

Founded: 1878
Former Names: Hurst FC and Rose Hill FC
Nickname: 'Robins'
Ground: Hurst Cross, Surrey Street, Ashton-Under-Lyne   OL6 8DY
Record Attendance: 11,000 (1952)

Colours: Shirts are Red and White halves, Black shorts
Telephone Nº: (0161) 339-4158
Fax Number: (0161) 339-4158
Ground Capacity: 4,500   **Seating Capacity**: 250
Pitch Size: 110 × 72 yards
Web site: www.ashtonutd.com

GENERAL INFORMATION
Car Parking: Street parking only
Coach Parking: At the ground
Nearest Railway Station: Ashton (1 mile)
Nearest Bus Station: Ashton
Club Shop: At the ground
Opening Times: Before and during matches only
Telephone Nº: (0161) 339-4158

GROUND INFORMATION
Away Supporters' Entrances: No usual segregation

ADMISSION INFO (2018/2019 PRICES)
Adult Standing/Seating: £12.00
Concessionary Standing/Seating: £8.00
Note: Under-5s admitted free with a paying adult
Programme Price: £2.00

DISABLED INFORMATION
Wheelchairs: Accommodated
Helpers: Please phone the club for information
Prices: Please phone the club for information
Disabled Toilets: Available
Contact: (0161) 339-4158 Please contact the club prior to the game to make necessary arrangements.

Travelling Supporters' Information:
Routes: From the M1: Exit at Juntion 35A and follow signs for Manchester A616. Follow A616 for 11 miles then turn left at roundabout towards Manchester on A628. Follow A638 for 14 miles, passing through Tintwistle and Hollingworth. At the first set of traffic lights at the Gunn Inn go straight on and up the hill for ½ mile. Bear right at the A6018 signposted Ashton-Under-Lyne, Stalybridge and Mossley. Follow for 3 miles, passing Stalybridge Celtic FC on the left. At the 4th set of traffic lights turn right just past the BP Garage. Continue up Ridge Hill Lane for 250 yards where the road bears left and becomes Darnton Road. Continue, passing boating lake and Hospital on the right. Continue through the lights signposted Oldham and go up the hill for ½ mile. * Turn left at the first set of traffic lights then immediately right for the ground; From the M60: Take M60 towards Stockport, exit at Junction 23 and turn left (signposted Ashton). After 100 yards turn right at traffic lights onto A635 towards Ashton. After ½ mile you will reach a roundabout with a Police Station on the left. Stay in the 2nd lane heading towards Stalybridge & Halifax (still A635). Go straight on at next roundabout with Asda on the right until the following roundabout. Take 2nd exit signposted A670 Tameside Hospital. After 500 yards turn right into Mossley Road and after 600 yards turn left at the traffic lights towards Oldham and continue up the hill for ½ mile. Then as from *.

BLYTH SPARTANS AFC

Founded: 1899
Former Names: None
Nickname: 'Spartans'
Ground: Croft Park, Blyth, Northumberland, NE24 3JE
Record Attendance: 10,186 (1956)
Pitch Size: 110 × 70 yards

Colours: Green and White striped shirts, Black shorts
Telephone Nº: (01670) 352373 (Office)
Fax Number: (01670) 545592
Ground Capacity: 4,185
Seating Capacity: 500
Web site: www.blythspartans.com

GENERAL INFORMATION

Car Parking: At the ground
Coach Parking: At the ground
Nearest Railway Station: Newcastle
Nearest Bus Station: Blyth (5 minutes walk)
Club Shop: At the ground
Opening Times: Matchdays only
Telephone Nº: (01670) 352373

GROUND INFORMATION

Away Supporters' Entrances & Sections:
No usual segregation

ADMISSION INFO (2018/2019 PRICES)

Adult Standing: £12.00   **Adult Seating**: £14.00
Senior Citizen Standing: £7.00
Senior Citizen Seating: £9.00
Ages 11 to 16 & Student Standing: £5.00
Ages 11 to 16 & Student Seating: £7.00
Note: Under-11s are admitted free of charge when accompanied by a paying adult
Programme Price: £2.00

DISABLED INFORMATION

Wheelchairs: Accommodated
Helpers: Please phone the club for information
Prices: Adult disabled fans are charged the Senior Citizen rate shown above. Younger disabled fans charged lower rate.
Disabled Toilets: Available
Contact: (01670) 352373 (Bookings are necessary)

Travelling Supporters' Information:
Routes: Pass through the Tyne Tunnel and take the left lane for Morpeth (A19/A1). At the 2nd roundabout (after approximately 7 miles) take full right turn for the A189 (signposted Ashington). After 2 miles take the slip road (A1061 signposted Blyth). Follow signs for Blyth turning left at the caravan site. At the 2nd roundabout turn right and the ground is on the left.

BOSTON UNITED FC

Founded: 1933
Former Names: Boston Town FC & Boston Swifts FC
Nickname: 'The Pilgrims'
Ground: Jakemans Stadium, York Street, Boston, PE21 6JN
Ground Capacity: 6,778 **Seating Capacity**: 4,708
Pitch Size: 112 × 72 yards
Record Attendance: 11,000 (vs Derby County, 1974)

Colours: Amber and Black shirts with Black shorts and Amber socks
Telephone Nº: (01205) 364406 (Office)
Matchday Info: (01205) 364406 or 07860 663299
Fax Number: (01205) 354063
Web Site: www.bostonunited.co.uk
E-mail: admin@bufc.co.uk

GENERAL INFORMATION
Car Parking: Permit holders only
Coach Parking: Available near to the ground
Nearest Railway Station: Boston (1 mile)
Nearest Bus Station: Boston Coach Station (¼ mile)
Club Shop: In the car park at the ground
Opening Times: Weekdays from 9.00am to 5.00pm and Saturday Matchdays from 11.00am to 5.00pm
Telephone Nº: (01205) 364406

GROUND INFORMATION
Away Supporters' Entrances & Sections:
York Street Entrances 3 & 4 (subject to a move to the Jakemans Stand if so advised by the police)

ADMISSION INFO (2018/2019 PRICES)
Adult Standing: £13.00   **Adult Seating**: £15.00
Child Standing: £4.00
Child Seating: £5.00
Senior Citizen Standing: £10.00
Senior Citizen Seating: £11.00
Note: A range of discounted Family tickets are also available.
Programme Price: £3.00

DISABLED INFORMATION
Wheelchairs: 7 spaces available for home fans, 4 spaces for away fans below the Main Stand at the Town End
Helpers: One helper admitted per disabled fan
Prices: £13.00 for the disabled. Free of charge for helpers
Disabled Toilets: Available in the Town End Terrace
Contact: (01205) 364406 (Bookings are necessary)

Travelling Supporters' Information:
From the North: Take the A17 from Sleaford, bear right after the railway crossing to the traffic lights over the bridge. Go forward through the traffic lights into York Street for the ground; From the South: Take the A16 from Spalding and turn right at the traffic lights over the bridge. Go forward through the next traffic lights into York Street for the ground.

BRACKLEY TOWN FC

Founded: 1890
Former Names: None
Nickname: 'Saints'
Ground: St. James Park, Churchill Way, Brackley, NN13 7EJ
Record Attendance: 2,604 (2012/13 season)

Colours: Red and White shirts with White shorts
Telephone Nº: (01280) 704077
Ground Capacity: 3,500
Seating Capacity: 300
Web Site: www.brackleytownfc.com
E-mail: janenebutters@brackleytownfc.co.uk

GENERAL INFORMATION

Car Parking: At the ground (£2.00 charge per car)
Coach Parking: At the ground
Nearest Railway Station: King's Sutton (6¾ miles)
Club Shop: At the ground
Opening Times: Matchdays and by appointment only
Telephone Nº: (01280) 704077

GROUND INFORMATION

Away Supporters' Entrances & Sections:
No usual segregation

ADMISSION INFO (2018/2019 PRICES)

Adult Standing: £12.00
Adult Seating: £12.00
Senior Citizen/Student Standing: £6.00
Senior Citizen/Student Seating: £6.00
Under-18s Standing: £3.00
Under-18s Seating: £3.00
Under-10s Seating/Standing: Free of charge

DISABLED INFORMATION

Wheelchairs: Accommodated
Helpers: Admitted
Prices: Normal prices apply for the disabled. Free for helpers
Disabled Toilets: Available
Contact: (01280) 704077 (Stephen Toghill – bookings are necessary)

Travelling Supporters' Information:
Routes: From the West: Take the A422 to Brackley and take the first exit at the roundabout with the junction of the A43, heading north into Oxford Road.* Go straight on at the next roundabout and continue into Bridge Street before turning right into Churchill Way. The ground is located at the end of the road; From the South: Take the A43 northwards to Brackley. Take the second exit at the roundabout with the junction of the A422 and head into Oxford Road. Then as from * above; From the North-East: Take the A43 to Brackley. Upon reaching Brackley, take the 1st exit at the 1st roundabout, the 2nd exit at the next roundabout then the 3rd exit at the following roundabout into Oxford Road. Then as from * above.

BRADFORD PARK AVENUE FC

Founded: 1907 (Re-formed in 1988)
Former Names: None
Nickname: 'Avenue'
Ground: Horsfall Stadium, Cemetery Road, Bradford, BD6 2NG
Ground Capacity: 3,500 **Seating Capacity**: 1,800
Record Attendance: 2,100 (2003)
Pitch Size: 112 × 71 yards

Colours: Green & White hooped shirts, White shorts
Telephone Nº: 07912 271498 (Ground)
Office Address: Hugh House, Foundry Street, Brighouse HD6 1LT
Office Number: (01484) 400007
Web site: www.bpafc.com
E-mail: joemosley@bpafc.com

GENERAL INFORMATION
Car Parking: Street parking and some spaces at the ground
Coach Parking: At the ground
Nearest Railway Station: Bradford Interchange (3 miles)
Nearest Bus Station: Bradford Interchange (3 miles)
Club Shop: At the ground
Opening Times: Matchdays only
Telephone Nº: –

GROUND INFORMATION
Away Supporters' Entrances & Sections:
Segregation only used when required

ADMISSION INFO (2018/2019 PRICES)
Adult Standing/Seating: £12.00
Senior Citizen Standing/Seating: £9.00
Student Standing/Seating: £7.00
Under-16s Standing/Seating: £2.00

DISABLED INFORMATION
Wheelchairs: Accommodated in front of the Stand
Helpers: Please phone the club for information
Prices: Please phone the club for information
Disabled Toilets: Available
Contact: – (Bookings are not necessary)

Travelling Supporters' Information:
Routes: Exit the M62 at Junction 26 and take the M606 to its end. At the roundabout go along the A6036 (signposted Halifax) and pass Odsal Stadium on the left. At the roundabout by Osdal take the 3rd exit (still A6036 Halifax). After just under 1 mile, turn left at the Kinderhaven Nursery into Cemetery Road. The ground is 150 yards on the left.

CHESTER FC

Founded: 1885
Former Names: Chester FC and Chester City FC
Nickname: 'Blues'
Ground: Swansway Chester Stadium, Bumpers Lane, Chester CH1 4LT
Pitch Size: 116 × 75 yards
Record Attendance: 5,987 (17th April 2004)

Colours: Blue and White striped shirts, White shorts
Ground Telephone N°: (01244) 371376
Ticket Office: (01244) 371376
Ground Capacity: 5,376
Seating Capacity: 4,170
Web site: www.chesterfc.com
E-mail: info@chesterfc.com

GENERAL INFORMATION

Car Parking: Ample spaces available at the ground (£2.00)
Coach Parking: Available at the ground
Nearest Railway Station: Chester (2 miles)
Nearest Bus Station: Chester (1½ miles)
Club Shop: At the ground
Opening Times: Weekdays & matchdays 10.00am–4.00pm
Telephone N°: (01244) 371376

GROUND INFORMATION

Away Supporters' Entrances & Sections:
South Stand for covered seating and also part of the West Stand

ADMISSION INFO (2018/2019 PRICES)

Adult Standing: £12.00   **Adult Seating**: £15.00
Senior Citizen/Concessions Standing: £10.00
Senior Citizen/Concessions Seating: £12.00
Ages 18 to 21 Seating/Standing: £10.00
Ages 5 to 17 Seating/Standing: £3.00
Ages 5 to 11 Seating: £1.00 in the Community Stand
Note: Under-5s are admitted free of charge

DISABLED INFORMATION

Wheelchairs: 32 spaces for wheelchairs (with 40 helpers) in the West Stand and East Stand
Helpers: Admitted
Prices: Normal prices for the disabled. Free for helpers
Disabled Toilets: Available in West and East Stands
Contact: (01244) 371376   (Bookings are necessary)

Travelling Supporters' Information:
Routes: From the North: Take the M56, A41 or A56 into the Town Centre and then follow Queensferry (A548) signs into Sealand Road. Turn left at the traffic lights by 'Tesco' into Bumpers Lane – the ground is ½ mile at the end of the road; From the East: Take the A54 or A51 into the Town Centre (then as North); From the South: Take the A41 or A483 into Town Centre (then as North); From the West: Take the A55, A494 or A548 and follow Queensferry signs towards Birkenhead (A494) and after 1¼ miles bear left onto the A548 (then as North); From the M6/M56 (Avoiding Town Centre): Take the M56 to Junction 16 (signposted Queensferry), turn left at the roundabout onto A5117, signposted Wales. At the next roundabout turn left onto the A5480 (signposted Chester) and after approximately 3 miles take the 3rd exit from the roundabout (signposted Sealand Road Industrial Parks). Go straight across 2 sets of traffic lights into Bumpers Lane. The ground is ½ mile on the right.

CHORLEY FC

Founded: 1883
Former Names: None
Nickname: 'Magpies'
Ground: The Chorley Group Victory Park Stadium, Duke Street, Chorley,   PR7 3DU
Record Attendance: 9,679 (1931/32 season)
Pitch Size: 112 × 72 yards

Colours: Black & White striped shirts with Black shorts
Telephone N°: (01257) 230007
Fax Number: (01257) 275662
Ground Capacity: 4,300
Seating Capacity: 900
Web site: www.chorleyfc.com
E-mail: info@chorleyfc.com

GENERAL INFORMATION

Car Parking: 80 spaces available at the ground (£3.00)
Coach Parking: At the ground
Nearest Railway Station: Chorley (¼ mile)
Nearest Bus Station: 15 minutes from the ground
Club Shop: At the ground
Opening Times: Weekdays 12.00pm to 2.00pm and Matchdays 12.00pm until kick-off.
Telephone N°: (01257) 230007

GROUND INFORMATION

Away Supporters' Entrances & Sections:
Pilling Lane Stand entrances and accommodation

ADMISSION INFO (2018/2019 PRICES)

Adult Standing: £12.00
Adult Seating: £12.00
Concessionary Standing/Seating: £9.00
Student (Ages 16 to 22) Standing/Seating: £7.00
Under-16s Standing/Seating: £5.00
Under-12s Standing/Seating: Free with a paying adult
Programme Price: £2.50

DISABLED INFORMATION

Wheelchairs: Accommodated by prior arrangement
Helpers: Please contact the club for information
Prices: Please contact the club for information
Disabled Toilets: Available in the Social Club
Contact: (01257) 230007   (Bookings are not necessary)

Travelling Supporters' Information:
Routes: Exit the M61 at Junction 6 and follow the A6 to Chorley. Going past the Yarrow Bridge Hotel on Bolton Road, turn left at the 1st set of traffic lights into Pilling Lane. Take the 1st right into Ashby Street and the ground is the 2nd entrance on the left; Alternative Route: Exit the M6 at Junction 27 and follow signs to Chorley. Turn left at the lights and continue down the A49 for 2½ miles before turning right onto B5251. On entering Chorley, turn right into Duke Street 200 yards past The Plough.

CURZON ASHTON FC

Founded: 1963
Former Names: None
Nickname: 'The Nash'
Ground: Tameside Stadium, Richmond Street, Ashton-under-Lyne   OL7 9HG
Record Attendance: 3,210 (2007)
Pitch Size: 114 × 72 yards

Colours: Royal Blue shirts and shorts
Telephone Nº: (0161) 330-6033
Fax Number: (0161) 339-8802
Ground Capacity: 4,000
Seating Capacity: 527
Web Site: www.curzon-ashton.co.uk
E-mail: rob@curzon-ashton.co.uk

GENERAL INFORMATION
Car Parking: At the ground
Coach Parking: At the ground
Nearest Railway Station: Ashton-under-Lyne (1 mile)
Club Shop: At the ground
Opening Times: Matchdays only
Telephone Nº: (0161) 330-6033

GROUND INFORMATION
Away Supporters' Entrances & Sections:
No usual segregation

ADMISSION INFO (2018/2019 PRICES)
Adult Standing: £12.00
Adult Seating: £12.00
Concessionary Standing: £6.00
Concessionary Seating: £6.00
Under-16s/Student Standing: £3.00
Under-16s/Student Seating: £3.00
Programme Price: £2.00

DISABLED INFORMATION
Wheelchairs: Accommodated
Helpers: Admitted
Prices: Normal prices apply for the disabled and helpers
Disabled Toilets: Available
Contact: (0161) 330-6033   (Bookings are not necessary)

Travelling Supporters' Information:
Routes: Exit the M60 at Junction 23 and take the A6140 signposted for Ashton. Continue along the A6140 to the set of traffic lights with a Cinema on the right then turn left. Cross over a bridge and go straight across the mini-roundabout before turning left into the ground. NOTE: Diversions may be in force during the 2010/2011 season due to bridge replacement work.

DARLINGTON FC

Founded: 1883 (Re-formed 2012)
Former Names: Successor to the club Darlington FC, formed as Darlington 1883 and renamed in 2017
Nickname: 'Darlo', 'The Quakers'
Ground: Blackwell Meadows, Grange Road, Darlington   DL1 5NR
Record Attendance: 3,000 (26th December 2016)
Pitch Size: 110 × 75 yards

Ground Capacity: 3,281
Seating Capacity: 588
Colours: Black and White hooped shirts, Black shorts
Contact Telephone Nº: None
Web Site: www.darlingtonfootballclub.co.uk
E-mail: rob.jones@darlingtonfc.org

GENERAL INFORMATION

Car Parking: A limited number of spaces at Blackwell Meadows are available on a first-come, first-served basis with a £5.00 fee. Alternatively, use town centre car parks (1½ miles)
Coach Parking: Limited parking at the ground
Nearest Railway Station: Darlington (1½ miles)
Nearest Bus Station: Darlington Town Centre (1½ miles)
Club Shop: At the Dolphin Centre in Darlington
Opening Times: Weekdays 10.00am to 1.00pm.
Telephone Nº: 07488 564642
E-mail: shop@dfc1883.co.uk

GROUND INFORMATION

Away Supporters' Entrances & Sections:
No usual segregation

ADMISSION INFO (2017/2018 PRICES)

Adult Standing: £14.00
Adult Seating: £14.00
Concessionary Standing/Seating: £10.00
Junior Standing/Seating (Ages 5–16): £5.00
Under-5s Standing/Seating: Free of charge
Please contact the club for 2018/2019 pricing information.
Programme Price: £2.50

DISABLED INFORMATION

Wheelchairs: Accommodated
Helpers: Helpers are admitted
Prices: Normal prices apply for the disabled and helpers
Disabled Toilets: Available
Contact: rob.jones@darlingtonfc.org   (Bookings are necessary)

Travelling Supporters' Information:
Routes: From the South: Exit the A1(M) at Junction 57 and take the A66(M) towards Darlington. At the end of the motorway, continue onto the A66 and take the second exit at the next roundabout onto the A167 Darlington Road. Blackwell Meadows is on the right after 400 yards; From the North: Exit the A1(M) at Junction 59 and take the A167 to Darlington. Upon entering Darlington, continue along the A167, taking the second exit at the roundabout into North Road, the first exit at Northgate Roundabout onto St. Cuthbert's Way then following the road around around Darlington town centre into Victoria Road before turning left at the Baptist church into Grange Road. Blackwell Meadows in on the left after approximately 1 mile.

FC UNITED OF MANCHESTER

Photo courtesy of John Mills @ Altius Photography

Founded: 2005
Nickname: 'F.C.'
Ground: Broadhurst Park, 310 Lightbowne Road, Moston, Manchester   M40 0FJ
Ground Capacity: 4,400
Seating Capacity: 750
Pitch Size: 110 × 71 yards

Record Attendance: 4,232 (29th May 2015)
Colours: Red shirts with White shorts
Telephone Nº: (0161) 769-2005
Fax Number: (0161) 769-2014
E-mail: office@fc-utd.co.uk
Web Site: www.fc-utd.co.uk

GENERAL INFORMATION

Car Parking: 160 spaces at the ground. Pre-booking only, £5.00 charge. Other car parks are located within ½ mile of Broadhurst Park. Check the club's web site for further details.
Coach Parking: Phone the club on (0161) 769-2005
Nearest Railway Station: Moston (¾ mile)
Nearest Bus Station: A number of services travel to the ground. Please check the club's web site for further details.
Club Shop: At the ground
Opening Times: Matchdays only
Telephone Nº: (0161) 769-2005

GROUND INFORMATION

Away Supporters' Entrances & Sections:
No usual segregation but away fans will be accommodated in the Lightbowne Road End if necessary.

ADMISSION INFO (2018/2019 PRICES)

Adult Seating: £12.00
Senior Citizen (Over-60s)/Student Seating: £7.00
Under-18s Seating: £3.00
Programme Price: £2.00

DISABLED INFORMATION

Wheelchairs: Spaces for wheelchairs are available in all areas of the ground
Helpers: One helper admitted per wheelchair
Prices: Normal prices for wheelchair users. Helpers are admitted free of charge.
Disabled Toilets: Available behind the Main Stand
Contact: (0161) 769-2005   (Bookings are not necessary)

Travelling Supporters' Information: From the M60 travelling clockwise: Exit the M60 at junction 20 and turn onto the A664. At the traffic signals turn left onto the A6104. Travel straight on and then at the Greengate roundabout take the 4th exit onto Lightbowne Road, the B6393. Carry straight on for around a half a mile and Broadhurst Park is on your left; From the M60 travelling anti-clockwise: Exit the M60 at junction 22, then straight on to Hollingwood Avenue, the A6104 . Travel straight on and then at the Greengate roundabout take the 1st exit onto Lightbowne Road, the B6393. Carry straight on for around a half a mile and Broadhurst Park is on your left.

GUISELEY AFC

Founded: 1909
Former Names: None
Nickname: 'The Lions'
Ground: Nethermoor Park, Otley Road, Guiseley, Leeds   LS20 8BT
Record Attendance: 2,486 (1989/90)
Pitch Size: 110 × 69 yards

Colours: White shirts with Navy Blue shorts
Telephone Nº: 07507 750553
Social Club Phone Nº: (01943) 872872
Fax Number: (01943) 873223
Ground Capacity: 4,000
Seating Capacity: 518
Web site: www.guiseleyafc.co.uk
E-mail: admin@guiseleyafc.co.uk

GENERAL INFORMATION

Car Parking: At the ground and in Netherfield Road – Please do not park in Ings Crescent!
Coach Parking: At the ground
Nearest Railway Station: Guiseley (5 minute walk)
Nearest Bus Station: Bus Stop outside the ground
Club Shop: At the ground
Opening Times: Matchdays only
Telephone Nº: (01943) 879236 (weekdays)
Postal Sales: Yes

GROUND INFORMATION

Away Supporters' Entrances & Sections:
No usual segregation

ADMISSION INFO (2018/2019 PRICES)

Adult Standing: £13.00
Adult Seating: £13.00
Concessionary Standing/Seating: £9.00
Ages 11 to 18 Standing/Seating: £5.00
Under-11s Standing/Seating: £1.00 when accompanied by a paying adult

DISABLED INFORMATION

Wheelchairs: Accommodated
Helpers: Admitted
Prices: Normal prices for disabled fans. Free for helpers
Disabled Toilets: None
Contact: (01943) 879236   (Bookings are advisable)

Travelling Supporters' Information:
Routes: Exit the M62 at Junction 28 and take the Leeds Ring Road to the roundabout at the junction of the A65 at Horsforth. Turn left onto the A65 and pass through Rawdon to Guiseley keeping Morrison's supermarket on your left. Pass straight through the traffic lights with the Station pub or your right and the ground is on the right after ¼ mile, adjacent to the cricket field.

HEREFORD FC

Founded: 1924
Former Names: None
Nickname: 'United' 'The Bulls'
Ground: Edgar Street, Hereford   HR4 9JU
Record Attendance: 18,114 (4th January 1958)
Pitch Size: 110 × 70 yards

Colours: White shirts with Black shorts
Telephone Nº: (01432) 268-257
Ground Capacity: 4,913
Seating Capacity: 3,390
Web site: www.herefordfc.co.uk
E-mail: info@herefordfc.co.uk

GENERAL INFORMATION

Car Parking: Merton Meadow Car Park (Near the ground)
Coach Parking: Merton Meadow Car Park
Nearest Railway Station: Hereford (½ mile)
Nearest Bus Station: Commercial Road, Hereford
Club Shop: At the ground
Opening Times: Wednesday and Friday 10.00am – 4.00pm.
Midweek home games, 10.00am–4.00pm & 6.00pm–7.30pm,
Saturday Matchdays 12.00pm to 2.45pm.
Telephone Nº: (01432) 268257

GROUND INFORMATION

Away Supporters' Entrances & Sections:
Edgar Street entrances for the Edgar Street Stand and Terrace

ADMISSION INFO (2018/2019 PRICES)

Adult Standing: £13.00
Adult Seating: £15.00
Ages 16 to 18 Standing: £7.00
Ages 16 to 18 Seating: £8.00
Under-16s Standing/Seating: £2.00 (Under-5s free)
Concessionary Standing: £12.00
Concessionary Seating: £14.00

DISABLED INFORMATION

Wheelchairs: 7 spaces in total for Home and Away fans in
the disabled section, Central Roofing Stand
Helpers: One helper admitted per disabled person
Prices: Concessionary prices for the disabled. Free for helpers
Disabled Toilets: Available
Contact: (01432) 268257   (Bookings are necessary)

Travelling Supporters' Information:
Routes: From the North: Follow A49 Hereford signs straight into Edgar Street; From the East: Take the A465 or A438 into
Hereford Town Centre, then follow signs for Leominster (A49) into Edgar Street; From the South: Take the A49 or A45 into the
Town Centre (then as East); From the West: Take the A438 into the Town Centre (then as East).

KIDDERMINSTER HARRIERS FC

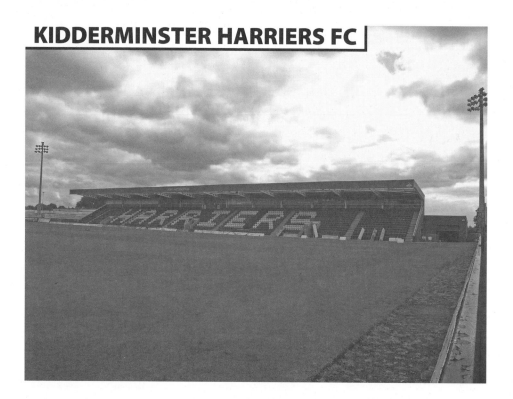

Founded: 1886
Nickname: 'Harriers'
Ground: Aggborough Stadium, Hoo Road, Kidderminster DY10 1NB
Ground Capacity: 6,444
Seating Capacity: 3,140
Record Attendance: 9,155 (1948)

Pitch Size: 110 × 72 yards
Colours: Red and White halved shirts, White shorts
Telephone Nº: (01562) 823931
Fax Number: (01562) 827329
Web Site: www.harriers.co.uk
E-mail: info@harriers.co.uk

GENERAL INFORMATION

Car Parking: At the ground (£3.00 to £5.00 per car)
Coach Parking: As directed
Nearest Railway Station: Kidderminster
Nearest Bus Station: Kidderminster Town Centre
Club Shop: At the ground
Opening Times: Weekdays 9.00am to 5.00pm and home Matchdays 10.30am to 5.30pm.
Telephone Nº: (01562) 823931

GROUND INFORMATION

Away Supporters' Entrances & Sections:
John Smiths Stand Entrance D and South Terrace Entrance E

ADMISSION INFO (2018/2019 PRICES)

Adult Standing: £15.00
Adult Seating: £17.00
Concessionary Standing: £9.00
Concessionary Seating: £12.00
Under-16s Standing: £3.00
Under-16s Seating: £5.00
Note: Under-5s are admitted free with a paying adult.

DISABLED INFORMATION

Wheelchairs: Home fans accommodated at the front of the Main Stand, Away fans in front of the John Smiths Stand
Helpers: Admitted
Prices: Normal prices for the disabled with one helper free
Disabled Toilets: Available by the disabled area
Contact: (01562) 823931 (Bookings are not necessary)

Travelling Supporters' Information:
Routes: Exit the M5 at Junction 3 and follow the A456 to Kidderminster. The ground is situated close by the Severn Valley Railway Station so follow the brown Steam Train signs and turn into Hoo Road about 200 yards downhill of the station. Follow the road along for ¼ mile and the ground is on the left.

LEAMINGTON FC

Founded: 1891
Former Names: Leamington Town FC, Lockheed Borg & Beck FC, AP Leamington FC and Lockheed Leamington FC
Nickname: 'The Brakes'
Ground: The Phillips 66 Community Stadium, Harbury Lane, Leamington Spa   CV33 9QB
Record Attendance: 2,102 (1st May 2017)

Colours: Gold and Black shirts with Black shorts
Telephone Nº: (01926) 430406
Fax Number: (01926) 430406
Ground Capacity: 3,000
Seating Capacity: 294
Web Site: www.leamingtonfc.co.uk
E-mail: info@leamingtonfc.co.uk

GENERAL INFORMATION
Car Parking: At the ground
Coach Parking: At the ground
Nearest Railway Station: Leamington (4 miles)
Club Shop: Please contact the club for information
Opening Times: Matchdays only
E-mail: shop@leamingtonfc.co.uk

GROUND INFORMATION
Away Supporters' Entrances & Sections:
No usual segregation

ADMISSION INFO (2018/2019 PRICES)
Adult Standing/Seating: £12.00
Concessionary Standing/Seating: £8.00
Under-18s Standing/Seating: £3.00 (Under-12s free)
Student Standing/Seating: £6.00

DISABLED INFORMATION
Wheelchairs: Accommodated
Helpers: Admitted
Prices: Normal prices apply for the disabled. Helpers are admitted free of charge
Disabled Toilets: Available
Contact: (01926) 430406 (Bookings are not necessary)

Travelling Supporters' Information:
Routes: Exit the M40 at Junction 14 and take the A452 towards Leamington continuing at the roundabout into Europa Way (still A452). After approximately ½ mile, take the 4th exit at the roundabout into Harbury Lane (signposted for Harbury and Bishops Tachbrook). Continue on Harbury lane, taking the 3rd exit at the first roundabout and going straight ahead at the traffic lights. The ground is on the left hand side of the road after approximately 1½ miles.   **SatNav**: CV33 9SA

NUNEATON TOWN FC

Founded: 1937 (Reformed 2008)
Former Names: Nuneaton Borough FC
Nickname: 'Boro'
Ground: Liberty Way, Attleborough Fields Industrial Estate, Nuneaton   CV11 6RR
Record Attendance: 3,480 (vs Luton Town, 2014)
Pitch Size: 109 × 74 yards

Colours: Blue shirts and white shorts
Telephone Nº: (024) 7638-5738
Fax Number: (024) 7637-2995
Ground Capacity: 4,614
Seating Capacity: 514
Web site: www.pitchero.com/clubs/nuneatontownfc
E-mail: admin@nuneatontownfc.com

GENERAL INFORMATION

Car Parking: On-site car park plus various other parking spaces available on the nearby Industrial Estate (£2.00 fee)
Coach Parking: At the ground (£10.00 fee)
Nearest Railway Station: Nuneaton (2 miles)
Nearest Bus Station: Nuneaton (2 miles)
Club Shop: Yes – The Boro Shop
Opening Times: By appointment and also on matchdays
Telephone Nº: (024) 7638-5738

GROUND INFORMATION

Away Supporters' Entrances & Sections:
No usual segregation

ADMISSION INFO (2018/2019 PRICES)

Adult Standing: £12.00
Adult Seating: £12.00
Concessionary Standing: £10.00
Concessionary Seating: £10.00
Ages 11 to 16 Standing/Seating: £3.00
Under-11s Standing Seating: Free with a paying adult

DISABLED INFORMATION

Wheelchairs: Accommodated, but only 5 spaces are available
Helpers: Admitted
Prices: Normal prices apply for the disabled and helpers
Disabled Toilets: Available
Contact: (024) 7638-5738   (Bookings are necessary)

Travelling Supporters' Information:
Routes: From the South, West and North-West: Exit the M6 at Junction 3 and follow the A444 into Nuneaton. At the Coton Arches roundabout turn right into Avenue Road which is the A4254 signposted for Hinckley. Continue along the A4254 following the road into Garrett Street then Eastboro Way then turn left into Townsend Drive. Follow the road round before turning left into Liberty Way for the ground; From the North: Exit the M1 at Junction 21 and follow the M69. Exit the M69 at Junction 1 and take the 4th exit at the roundabout onto the A5 (Tamworth, Nuneaton). At Longshoot Junction, turn left onto the A47, continue to the roundabout and take the 1st exit onto A4254 Eastborough Way. Turn right at the next roundabout into Townsend Drive then immediately right again for Liberty Way.

SOUTHPORT FC

Founded: 1881
Former Names: Southport Vulcan FC, Southport Central FC
Nickname: 'The Sandgrounders' and 'The Port'
Ground: Merseyrail Community Stadium, Haig Avenue, Southport, Merseyside   PR8 6JZ
Record Attendance: 20,010 (1932)
Pitch Size: 110 × 77 yards

Colours: Yellow shirts and shorts
Telephone Nº: (01704) 533422
Fax Number: (01704) 533455
Ground Capacity: 6,008
Seating Capacity: 1,660
Web site: www.southportfc.net

GENERAL INFORMATION
Car Parking: Street parking
Coach Parking: Adjacent to the ground
Nearest Railway Station: Meols Cop (½ mile)
Nearest Bus Station: Southport Town Centre
Club Shop: At the ground
Opening Times: Matchdays from 1.30pm (from 6.30pm on evening matchdays)
Telephone Nº: (01704) 533422

GROUND INFORMATION
Away Supporters' Entrances & Sections:
Blowick End entrances

ADMISSION INFO (2018/2019 PRICES)
Adult Standing: £13.50
Adult Seating: £15.00
Concessionary Standing: £10.00
Concessionary Seating: £11.00
Under-19s Standing/Seating: £5.00
Note: Children aged 11 and under are admitted free of charge when accompanied by a paying adult.

DISABLED INFORMATION
Wheelchairs: Accommodated in front of the Grandstand
Helpers: Admitted
Prices: Concessionary prices charged for the disabled. Helpers are admitted free of charge
Disabled Toilets: Available at the Blowick End of the Grandstand
Contact: (01704) 533422   (Bookings are not necessary)

Travelling Supporters' Information:
Routes: Exit the M58 at Junction 3 and take the A570 to Southport. At the major roundabout (McDonalds/Tesco) go straight on into Scarisbrick New Road, pass over the brook and turn right into Haig Avenue at the traffic lights. The ground is then on the right-hand side.

SPENNYMOOR TOWN FC

Founded: 2005 (Formed by the amalgamation of Evenwood Town and the defunct Spennymoor United)
Former Names: None
Nickname: 'The Moors'
Ground: The Brewery Field, Wood Vue, Spennymoor, Co. Durham   DL16 6JN
Record Attendance: 7,202 (30th March 1957)

Pitch Size: 104 × 65 yards
Colours: Black and White striped shirts, Black shorts
Telephone Nº: (01388) 827248
Ground Capacity: 3,000
Seating Capacity: 226
Web Site: www.spennymoortownfc.co.uk

GENERAL INFORMATION

Car Parking: Street parking sometimes available but it can get very congested so fans are recommended to use the car parks behind the Town Hall or Leisure Centre.
Coach Parking: Please contact Steven Lawson on 07871 206474 for information
Nearest Railway Station: Durham (6 miles)
Nearest Bus Station: Durham – the No.6 bus which stops in Durham Road, Spennymoor (15 minute journey)
Club Shop: At the ground
Opening Times: Matchdays only

GROUND INFORMATION

Away Supporters' Entrances & Sections:
No usual segregation

ADMISSION INFO (2018/2019 PRICES)

Adult Standing/Seating: £14.00
Over-60s Standing/Seating: £9.00
Under-18s Standing/Seating: £4.00
Note: Under-10s are admitted free with a paying adult
Programme Price: £2.50

DISABLED INFORMATION

Wheelchairs: Accommodated by arrangement. Entrance via the Wood Vue turnstiles
Helpers: One helper admitted per wheelchair
Prices: Normal prices are charged for fans with disabilities. Helpers are admitted free of charge
Disabled Toilets: Available
Contact: 07871 206474 (Steven Lawson)

Travelling Supporters' Information:
Routes: Exit the A1(M) at Junction 60 and follow the A689 to Rushyford. Take the 3rd exit at the Rushyford roundabout onto the A167 then the 3rd exit at the Chilton roundabout, continuing on the A167 towards Spennymoor. Take the first exit at the Thinford roundabout onto the A688, carry straight on at the small roundabout then take the 3rd exit at the next roundabout into St. Andrew's Lane. Continue along St. Andrew's Lane, turning left at the first roundabout then take the 2nd exit at the mini-roundabout, passing Asda into King Street, and the 2nd exit at the next mini-roundabout into Durham Road. Bear right along Durham Road and Wood Vue is on the left after a short distance.

STOCKPORT COUNTY FC

Photohraph courtesy of Mike Petch – Mphotographic.co.uk

Founded: 1883
Former Names: Heaton Norris Rovers FC
Nickname: 'Hatters' 'County'
Ground: Edgeley Park, Hardcastle Road, Edgeley, Stockport SK3 9DD
Ground Capacity: 10,841 (All seats)
Record Attendance: 27,833 (11th February 1950)
Pitch Size: 111 × 72 yards

Colours: Blue shirts and shorts
Telephone Nº: (0161) 266-2700
Ticket Office: (0161) 266-2700
Web Site: www.stockportcounty.com
E-mail: info@stockportcounty.com

GENERAL INFORMATION
Car Parking: Booth Street (nearby) £4.00
Coach Parking: Booth Street (£20.00)
Nearest Railway Station: Stockport (5 minutes walk)
Nearest Bus Station: Mersey Square (10 minutes walk)
Club Shop: At the ground
Opening Times: Monday to Friday from 12.00pm–4.00pm. Open until 7.45pm on matchdays during the week and also on Saturday matchdays 10.00am – 3.00pm then for 30 minutes after the game.
Telephone Nº: (0161) 266-2700

GROUND INFORMATION
Away Supporters' Entrances & Sections:
Railway End turnstiles for Railway End or turnstiles for Popular Side depending on the opponents

ADMISSION INFO (2018/2019 PRICES)
Adult Seating: £15.00
Concessionary Seating: £10.00
Under-18s Seating: £5.00
Senior Citizen Seating: £10.00
Note: Children under the age of 6 are admitted free.

DISABLED INFORMATION
Wheelchairs: 16 spaces in total. 10 in the Hardcastle Road Stand, 6 in the Cheadle Stand
Helpers: One helper admitted per disabled fan
Prices: £10.00 for the disabled. Helpers free of charge
Disabled Toilets: Yes
Contact: (0161) 266-2700 (Bookings are necessary)

Travelling Supporters' Information:
Routes: From the North, South and West: Exit the M60 at Junction 1 and join the A560, following signs for Cheadle. After ¼ mile turn right into Edgeley Road and after 1 mile turn right into Caroline Street for the ground; From the East: Take the A6 or A560 into Stockport Town Centre and turn left into Greek Street. Take the 2nd exit into Mercian Way (from the roundabout) then turn left into Caroline Street – the ground is straight ahead.

YORK CITY FC

Founded: 1922   (**Re-entered League**: 2012)
Nickname: 'The Minstermen'
Ground: Bootham Crescent, York   YO30 7AQ
Ground Capacity: 8,256
Seating Capacity: 3,409
Record Attendance: 28,123 (5th March 1938)
Pitch Size: 115 × 74 yards

Colours: Red shirts with Blue shorts
Telephone Nº: (01904) 559503
Ticket Office: (01904) 559503 Extension 1
Fax Number: (01904) 631457
Web Site: www.yorkcityfootballclub.co.uk
E-mail: enquiries@yorkcityfootballclub.co.uk

GENERAL INFORMATION

Car Parking: Spaces are available in York Hospital car park (5 minutes walk) from 1.00pm (Saturday matches) and from 5.45pm (midweek matches). A voucher must be downloaded from the club's website to purchase a ticket and cost is £2.50.
Coach Parking: By Police direction
Nearest Railway Station: York (1 mile)
Club Shop: At the ground
Opening Times: Weekdays 12.00am – 5.00pm; Saturday Matchdays 1.00pm–3.00pm and 4.40pm–5.30pm; Evening matches open from 6.00pm
Telephone Nº: (01904) 559503

GROUND INFORMATION

Away Supporters' Entrances & Sections:
Grosvenor Road turnstiles for Grosvenor Road End

ADMISSION INFO (2018/2019 PRICES)

Adult Standing: £14.00
Adult Seating: £15.00 – £17.00
Concessionary Standing: £12.00
Concessionary Seating: £10.00 – £12.00
Under-18s Standing/Seating: £6.00   (Under-5s free)
Programme Price: £3.00

DISABLED INFORMATION

Wheelchairs: 18 spaces in total for Home and Away fans in the disabled section, in front of the Pitchside Bar
Helpers: One helper admitted per disabled person
Prices: £6.00 – £14.00 for fans with disabilities. Helpers are admitted free of charge
Disabled Toilets: Available at entrance to the disabled area
Contact: (01904) 624447 (Ext. 1) (Bookings not necessary)

Travelling Supporters' Information:
Routes: From the North: Take the A1 then the A59 following signs for York. Cross the railway bridge and turn left after 2 miles into Water End. Turn right at the end following City Centre signs for nearly ½ mile then turn left into Bootham Crescent; From the South: Take the A64 and turn left after Buckles Inn onto the Outer Ring Road. Turn right onto the A19, follow City Centre signs for 1½ miles then turn left into Bootham Crescent; From the East: Take the Outer Ring Road turning left onto the A19. Then as from the South; From the West: Take the Outer Ring Road turning right onto the A19. Then as from the South.

THE VANARAMA NATIONAL LEAGUE SOUTH

Address

4th Floor, 20 Waterloo Street, Birmingham   B2   5TB

Phone   (0121) 643-3143

Web site   www.footballconference.co.uk

Clubs for the 2018/2019 Season

BATH CITY FC

Founded: 1889
Former Names: Bath AFC, Bath Railway FC and Bath Amateurs FC
Nickname: 'The Romans'
Ground: Twerton Park, Bath   BA2 1DB
Record Attendance: 18,020 (1960)
Pitch Size: 110 × 76 yards

Colours: Black and White striped shirts, Black shorts
Telephone Nº: (01225) 423087
Ground Capacity: 8,880
Seating Capacity: 1,006
Web site: www.bathcityfc.com
E-mail: info@bathcityfootballclub.co.uk

GENERAL INFORMATION
Car Parking: 150 spaces available at the ground
Coach Parking: Available at the ground
Nearest Railway Station: Oldfield Park (1 mile)
Nearest Bus Station: Dorchester Street, Bath
Club Shop: Yes – c/o Club
Opening Times: Matchdays and office hours
Telephone Nº: (01225) 423087

GROUND INFORMATION
Away Supporters' Entrances & Sections: Turnstiles 17-19

ADMISSION INFO (2018/2019 PRICES)
Adult Standing/Seating: £13.00
Senior Citizen Standing/Seating: £10.00
Students/Under-18s Standing/Seating: £7.00
Under-16s Standing/Seating: £2.00

DISABLED INFORMATION
Wheelchairs: 10 spaces available each for home and away fans in front of the Family Stand
Helpers: Admitted
Prices: Normal prices for the disabled. Free for helpers
Disabled Toilets: Available behind the Family Stand
Contact: (01225) 423087   (Bookings are necessary)

Travelling Supporters' Information:
Route: As a recommendation, avoid exiting the M4 at Junction 18 as the road takes you through Bath City Centre. Instead, exit the M4 at Junction 19 onto the M32. Turn off the M32 at Junction 1 and follow the A4174 Bristol Ring Road south then join the A4 for Bath. On the A4, after passing through Saltford you will reach a roundabout shortly before entering Bath. Take the 2nd exit at this roundabout then follow the road before turning left into Newton Road at the bottom of the steep hill. The ground is then on the right hand side of the road.

BILLERICAY TOWN FC

Founded: 1880
Former Names: None
Nickname: 'Town' 'Blues'
Ground: New Lodge, Blunts Wall Road, Billericay, Essex CM12 9SA
Ground Capacity: 5,000   **Seating Capacity**: 2,000
Record Attendance: 4,582 (vs West Ham, 2017)

Colours: Shirts are Royal Blue with White trim, shorts are White with Royal Blue trim
Telephone Nº: (01277) 652188 or 286474
Fax Number: (01277) 652188
Web site: www.billericaytownfc.co.uk
E-mail: info@billericaytownfc.co.uk

GENERAL INFORMATION
Car Parking: Please contact the club for information
Coach Parking: Please contact the club for information
Nearest Railway Station: Billericay (½ mile)
Club Shop: At the ground
Opening Times: Matchdays only

GROUND INFORMATION
Away Supporters' Entrances & Sections:
No usual segregation

ADMISSION INFO (2018/2019 PRICES)
Adult Standing/Seating: £13.00
Senior Citizen & Student Standing/Seating: £9.00
Ages 12 to 17 Standing/Seating: £5.00
Under-12s Standing/Seating: £1.00
Family Ticket: £25.00 (2 adults + 2 Under-11s)

DISABLED INFORMATION
Wheelchairs: Accommodated
Helpers: Admitted
Prices: Same prices as standing admission
Disabled Toilets: Available in the Clubhouse
Contact: (01277) 652188   (Bookings are necessary)

Travelling Supporters' Information:
Route: Exit the M25 at Junction 28 and follow the A129 to Billericay. Turn right at the 1st set of traffic lights into Tye Common Road then 2nd right into Blunts Wall Road and the ground is on the right.
Alternative route: Exit the M25 at Junction 29 and take the A129 road from Basildon into Billericay and turn left at the 2nd set of traffic lights into Tye Common Road. Then as above.

CHELMSFORD CITY FC

Founded: 1938
Former Names: Chelmsford FC
Nickname: 'City' or 'Clarets'
Ground: Melbourne Community Stadium, Salerno Way, Chelmsford   CM1 2EH
Record Attendance: 16,807 (at previous ground)
Pitch Size: 109 × 70 yards

Colours: Claret and White shirts and shorts
Telephone Nº: (01245) 290959
Ground Capacity: 3,000
Seating Capacity: 1,400
Web site: www.chelmsfordcityfc.com
E-mail: enquiries@chelmsfordcityfc.com

GENERAL INFORMATION

Car Parking: Limited space at ground and street parking
Coach Parking: Two spaces available at the ground subject to advance notice
Nearest Railway Station: Chelmsford (2 miles)
Nearest Bus Station: Chelmsford (2 miles)
Club Shop: At the ground
Opening Times: Matchdays only at present
Telephone Nº: (01245) 290959

GROUND INFORMATION

Away Supporters' Entrances & Sections:
No usual segregation

ADMISSION INFO (2018/2019 PRICES)

Adult Standing: £15.00
Adult Seating: £15.00
Under-18s Standing: £5.00
Under-18s Seating: £5.00
Under-12s Standing: Free of charge
Under-12s Seating: Free of charge
Concessionary Standing: £10.00
Concessionary Seating: £10.00

DISABLED INFORMATION

Wheelchairs: Spaces for 11 wheelchairs available
Helpers: Admitted free of charge
Prices: Disabled fans are charged standing admission prices
Disabled Toilets: Available
Contact: (01245) 290959   (Bookings are necessary)

Travelling Supporters' Information:
Route: The ground is situated next to the only set of high rise flats in Chelmsford which can therefore be used as a landmark. From the A12 from London: Exit the A12 at Junction 15 signposted for Chelmsford/Harlow/A414 and head towards Chelmsford along the dual-carriageway. At the third roundabout, immediately after passing the 'Superbowl' on the left, take the first exit into Westway, signposted for the Crematorium and Widford Industrial Estate. Continue along Westway which becomes Waterhouse Lane after the second set of traffic lights. At the next set of lights (at the gyratory system) take the first exit into Rainsford Road, signposted for Sawbridgeworth A1060. Continue along Rainsford Road then turn right into Chignal Road at the second set of traffic lights. Turn right again into Melbourne Avenue and Salerno Way is on the left at the end of the football pitches.

CHIPPENHAM TOWN FC

Founded: 1873
Former Names: None
Nickname: 'The Bluebirds'
Ground: Hardenhuish Park, Bristol Road, Chippenham, Wiltshire SN14 6LR
Record Attendance: 4,800 (1951)
Pitch Size: 110 × 70 yards

Colours: Royal Blue & White shirts, Royal Blue shorts
Telephone Nº: (01249) 650400
Contact Nº: (01793) 855518
Fax Number: (01249) 650400
Ground Capacity: 3,000
Seating Capacity: 300
Web site: www.pitchero.com/clubs/chippenhamtown

GENERAL INFORMATION

Car Parking: Adjacent to the ground
Coach Parking: At the ground
Nearest Railway Station: Chippenham (1 mile)
Nearest Bus Station: Chippenham
Club Shop: At the ground
Opening Times: Matchdays only
Telephone Nº: –

GROUND INFORMATION

Away Supporters' Entrances & Sections:
No usual segregation

ADMISSION INFO (2018/2019 PRICES)

Adult Standing: £10.00
Adult Seating: £11.00
Concessionary Standing: £6.00
Concessionary Seating: £7.00
Under-18s Standing: £3.00
Under-18s Seating: £4.00
Programme Price: £2.00

DISABLED INFORMATION

Wheelchairs: Accommodated at front of Stand
Helpers: Admitted
Prices: Normal prices apply for the disabled. Free for helpers
Disabled Toilets: None
Contact: (01249) 650400   (Bookings are not necessary)

Travelling Supporters' Information:
Routes: Exit the M4 at Junction 17 and take the A350. Turn right at the first roundabout and follow the road to the junction with the A420. Turn left following 'Town Centre' signs and the ground is just over ½ mile on the left near the Pelican crossing.

CONCORD RANGERS FC

Founded: 1967
Former Names: None
Nickname: 'The Beachboys'
Ground: Aspect Arena, Thames Road, Canvey Island, SS8 0HH
Record Attendance: 1,537 (vs Mansfield Town, 2014)

Colours: Yellow shirts with Yellow shorts
Telephone N°: (01268) 515750
Ground Capacity: 3,250
Seating Capacity: 375
Web Site: www.concordrangers.co.uk
E-mail: media@concordrangers.co.uk

GENERAL INFORMATION
Car Parking: At the ground
Coach Parking: At the ground
Nearest Railway Station: Benfleet
Club Shop: Available via the club's web site shortly
Opening Times: –
Telephone N°: –

GROUND INFORMATION
Away Supporters' Entrances & Sections:
No usual segregation

ADMISSION INFO (2018/2019 PRICES)
Adult Standing: £12.00
Adult Seating: £12.00
Senior Citizen Standing: £7.00
Senior Citizen Seating: £7.00
Ages 12 to 16 Standing/Seating: £3.00
Under-12s Standing/Seating: Free of charge

DISABLED INFORMATION
Wheelchairs: Accommodated
Helpers: Admitted
Prices: Normal prices apply for the disabled and helpers
Disabled Toilets: Available
Contact: (01268) 515750   (Bookings are necessary)

Travelling Supporters' Information:
Routes: Take the A13 to the A130 (Canvey Way) for Canvey Island. At the Benfleet roundabout, take the 3rd exit into Canvey Road and continue along through Charfleets Service Road into Long Road. Take the 5th turn on the right into Thorney Bay Road and Thames Road is the 3rd turn on the right. The ground is on the left-hand side around 300 yards down Thames Road.

DARTFORD FC

Founded: 1888
Former Names: None
Nickname: 'The Darts'
Ground: Princes Park Stadium, Grassbanks, Darenth Road, Dartford   DA1 1RT
Record Attendance: 4,097 (11th November 2006)
Pitch Size: 110 × 71 yards

Colours: White Shirts with Black Shorts
Telephone Nº: (01322) 299990
Fax Number: (01322) 299996
Ground Capacity: 4,118
Seating Capacity: 640
Web Site: www.dartfordfc.com
E-mail: info@dartfordfc.com

GENERAL INFORMATION
Car Parking: At the ground
Coach Parking: At the ground
Nearest Railway Station: Dartford (½ mile)
Nearest Bus Station: Dartford (½ mile) & Bluewater (2 miles)
Club Shop: At the ground
Opening Times: Matchdays only – 1.00pm to 6.00pm (but the stadium itself is open daily).
Telephone Nº: (01322) 299990

ADMISSION INFO (2018/2019 PRICES)
Adult Standing: £14.00
Adult Seating: £14.00
Senior Citizen/Concessionary Standing: £9.00
Senior Citizen/Concessionary Seating: £9.00
Youth (Ages 13 to 17) Standing/Seating: £5.00
Junior (Ages 5 to 12) Standing/Seating: £2.00
Under-5s Standing/Seating: Free of charge

DISABLED INFORMATION
Wheelchairs: Accommodated
Helpers: Admitted
Prices: Normal prices for the disabled. Free for helpers
Disabled Toilets: Available
Contact: (01322) 299991   (Bookings are not necessary)

Travelling Supporters' Information:
Routes: From M25 Clockwise: Exit the M25 at Junction 1B. At the roundabout, take the 3rd exit onto Princes Road (A225) then the second exit at the next roundabout.* Continue downhill to the traffic lights (with the ground on the left), turn left into Darenth Road then take the 2nd left for the Car Park; From M25 Anti-clockwise: Exit the M25 at Junction 2 and follow the A225 to the roundabout. Take the first exit at this roundabout then the 2nd exit at the next roundabout. Then as from * above.

DULWICH HAMLET FC

Dulwich & Hamlet are groundsharing with Tooting & Mitcham United FC for the 2018/2019 season.

Founded: 1893
Former Names: None
Nickname: 'The Hamlet'
Ground: Imperial Fields, Bishopsford Road, Morden, SM4 6BF
Record Attendance: 1,835 (at Champion Hill, 1998)
Pitch Size: 110 × 70 yards

Colours: Pink and Navy Blue quartered shirts with Navy Blue shorts
Telephone Nº: 07967 212353
Ground Capacity: 3,500
Seating Capacity: 612
Web site: www.pitchero.com/clubs/dulwichhamlet
E-mail: dhfc1893@yahoo.com

GENERAL INFORMATION

Car Parking: Approximately 150 spaces available at the ground and also street parking nearby
Coach Parking: At the ground
Nearest Railway Station: Mitcham Junction (1½ miles)
Nearest Tube Station: Morden (1½ miles)
Club Shop: At the ground and online at www.dhst.org.uk
Opening Times: Matchdays only

GROUND INFORMATION

Away Supporters' Entrances & Sections:
No usual segregation

ADMISSION INFO (2018/2019 PRICES)

Adult Standing: £12.00
Adult Seating: £12.00
Concessionary Standing: £5.00
Concessionary Seating: £5.00
Note: Under-13s are admitted free of charge when accompanying a paying adult

DISABLED INFORMATION

Wheelchairs: Accommodated with a lift available for the different levels of the stand
Helpers: Admitted
Prices: Concessionary prices for disabled fans with one helper admitted free with each.
Disabled Toilets: Available
Contact: 07967 212353 (Bookings are necessary)

Travelling Supporters' Information:
Routes: Exit the M25 at Junction 8 and take the A217 towards London. At the major Rose Hill Roundabout (which also has traffic lights), take the 3rd exit for Mitcham which is still the A217 but is named Bishopsford Road. Continue for about a mile, passing through two sets of traffic lights and the ground is situated on the right, opposite a petrol station.

EASTBOURNE BOROUGH FC

Founded: 1963
Former Names: Langney Sports FC
Nickname: 'The Sports'
Ground: Langney Sports Club, Priory Lane, Langney, Eastbourne   BN23 7QH
Record Attendance: 3,770 (5th November 2005)
Pitch Size: 115 × 72 yards

Colours: Red shirts with Red and Black shorts
Telephone Nº: (01323) 766265
Fax Number: (01323) 741627
Ground Capacity: 4,400
Seating Capacity: 542
Web site: www.ebfc.co.uk
E-mail: info@ebfc.co.uk

GENERAL INFORMATION

Car Parking: Around 400 spaces available at the ground
Coach Parking: At the ground
Nearest Railway Station: Eastbourne (3 miles)
Nearest Bus Station: Eastbourne   (Service 6A to ground)
Club Shop: At the ground
Opening Times: Matchdays only
Telephone Nº: (01323) 766265

GROUND INFORMATION

Away Supporters' Entrances & Sections:
No usual segregation

ADMISSION INFO (2018/2019 PRICES)

Adult Standing: £13.00
Adult Seating: £13.00
Concessionary Standing/Seating: £9.00
Student Standing/Seating: £5.00
Under-18s Standing/Seating: £1.00

DISABLED INFORMATION

Wheelchairs: 6 spaces available
Helpers: Admitted
Prices: Normal prices apply for fans with disabilities. Free of charge for helpers
Disabled Toilets: Available
Contact: (01323) 766265   (Bookings are necessary)

Travelling Supporters' Information:
Routes: From the North: Exit the A22 onto the Polegate bypass, signposted A27 Eastbourne, Hastings & Bexhill. *Take the 2nd exit at the next roundabout for Stone Cross and Westham (A22) then the first exit at the following roundabout signposted Stone Cross and Westham. Turn right after ½ mile into Friday Street (B2104). At the end of Friday Street, turn left at the double mini-roundabout into Hide Hollow (B2191), passing Eastbourne Crematorium on your right. Turn right at the roundabout into Priory Road, and Priory Lane is about 200 yards down the road on the left; Approaching on the A27 from Brighton: Turn left at the Polegate traffic lights then take 2nd exit at the large roundabout to join the bypass. Then as from *.

EAST THURROCK UNITED FC

Founded: 1969
Former Names: None
Nickname: 'The Rocks'
Ground: FutureFuel Stadium, Rookery Hill, Corringham, Essex, SS17 9LB
Record Attendance: 1,661 (vs Dulwich Hamlet, 2016)
Pitch Size: 110 × 72 yards

Colours: Amber shirts with Black shorts
Telephone Nº: (01375) 644166
Ground Capacity: 3,500
Seating Capacity: 160
Web: www.pitchero.com/clubs/eastthurrockunited

GENERAL INFORMATION

Car Parking: Spaces for 250 cars at the ground
Coach Parking: At the ground
Nearest Railway Station: Stanford-le-Hope (2 miles)
Nearest Bus Station: Stanford-le-Hope (2 miles)
Club Shop: At the ground
Opening Times: Matchdays only

GROUND INFORMATION

Away Supporters' Entrances & Sections:
No usual segregation

ADMISSION INFO (2018/2019 PRICES)

Adult Standing: £13.00
Adult Seating: £13.00
Concessionary Standing/Seating: £6.00
Under-16s Standing/Seating: £3.00
Family Tickets: £25.00 (2 adults + 2 Under-16s)

DISABLED INFORMATION

Wheelchairs: Accommodated
Helpers: Admitted
Prices: Standard prices apply
Disabled Toilets: Available
Contact: 07885 313435 (Bookings are necessary)

Travelling Supporters' Information:
Routes: Exit the M25 at Junction 30 and follow the A13 East. At Stanford-le-Hope turn-off on to the A1014 Coryton, cross over the roundabout and pass through the traffic lights. Then take the first turning on the left signposted Corringham and the ground is immediately on the left.

GLOUCESTER CITY AFC

Gloucester City are groundsharing with Evesham United during the 2018/2019 season.

Unfortunately, no photograph of the stadium was available at the time of going to press.

Founded: 1889 (**Re-formed**: 1980)
Forner Names: Gloucester YMCA
Nickname: 'The Tigers'
Ground: The Spiers and Hartwell Jubilee Stadium, Cheltenham Road, Evesham WR11 3LZ
Ground Capacity: 3,000
Seating Capacity: 300

Record Attendance: 8,326 (1956)
Pitch Size: 110 × 72 yards
Colours: Yellow and Black Striped shirts, Black shorts
Telephone Nº: 07704 923819
Web Site: www.gloucestercityafc.com
E-mail: contact@gloucestercityafc.com

GENERAL INFORMATION
Car Parking: Available at the ground.
Coach Parking: At the ground
Nearest Railway Station: Evesham (1¾ miles)
Nearest Bus Station: Evesham (1½ miles)
Club Shop: At the ground
Opening Times: Matchdays only

GROUND INFORMATION
Away Supporters' Entrances & Sections:
No usual segregation

ADMISSION INFO (2018/2019 PRICES)
Adult Standing: £13.00
Adult Seating: £13.00
Under-16s Standing: Free of charge
Under-16s Seating: Free of charge
Concessionary Standing: £7.00
Concessionary Seating: £7.00

DISABLED INFORMATION
Wheelchairs: Accommodated
Helpers: Admitted free of charge
Prices: Normal prices apply for disabled fans
Disabled Toilets: Available
Contact: 07704 923819 (Chris Gage)

Travelling Supporters' Information:
Routes: From the North: Exit the M5 at Junction 7 and follow the B4084 through Pershore into Evesham. At the traffic lights with the River Avon and Bridge on the left, turn right into Cheltenham Road then continue through two sets of traffic lights passing the Tesco Garage and Ambulance Station on the left before reaching a roundabout. The ground is then on the right; From the South: Exit the M5 at Junction 9, take the 3rd exit and follow the A46 to Evesham. The ground is on the left by the roundabout on outskirts of Evesham; From the East: Take the A44 to Evesham then turn left onto the A46 at the roundabout on the outskirts of Evesham. Continue over the next roundabout passing the Strawberry Field public house and McDonalds on the right and the ground is straight on at the next roundabout.

HAMPTON & RICHMOND BOROUGH FC

Founded: 1921
Former Names: Hampton FC
Nickname: 'Beavers'
Ground: Beveree Stadium, Beaver Close, off Station Road, Hampton, Middlesex   TW12 2BX
Record Attendance: 3,225   (vs AFC Wimbledon, 2009)
Pitch Size: 113 × 71 yards

Colours: Blue and Red Striped shirts with Red shorts
Matchday Phone Nº: (020) 8979-2456
Fax Number: (020) 8979-2456
Ground Capacity: 3,500
Seating Capacity: 300
Web site: www.hamptonfc.net

GENERAL INFORMATION
Car Parking: At the ground and street parking
Coach Parking: Contact the Club for information
Nearest Railway Station: Hampton
Nearest Bus Station: Hounslow/Kingston/Fulwell
Club Shop: At the ground
Opening Times: Matchdays only
Telephone Nº: None

GROUND INFORMATION
Away Supporters' Entrances & Sections:
No usual segregation

ADMISSION INFO (2018/2019 PRICES)
Adult Standing: £13.00
Adult Seating: £13.00
Senior Citizen/Concessionary Standing: £8.00
Senior Citizen/Concessionary Seating: £8.00
Under-16s Standing/Seating: £3.00
Note: Under-5s are admitted free of charge
Programme Price: £2.50

DISABLED INFORMATION
Wheelchairs: Accommodated
Helpers: Admitted
Prices: Normal prices apply
Disabled Toilets: Available
Contact: (020) 8979-2456   (Bookings are not necessary)

Travelling Supporters' Information:
Routes: From the South: Exit the M3 at Junction 1 and follow the A308 (signposted Kingston). Turn 1st left after Kempton Park into Percy Road. Turn right at the level crossing into Station Road then left into Beaver Close for the ground; From the North: Take the A305 from Twickenham then turn left onto the A311. Pass through Hampton Hill onto Hampton High Street. Turn right at the White Hart pub (just before the junction with the A308), then right into Station Road and right again into Beaver Close.

HEMEL HEMPSTEAD TOWN FC

Founded: 1885
Former Names: Apsley FC and Hemel Hempstead FC
Nickname: 'The Tudors'
Ground: Vauxhall Road, Adeyfield, Hemel Hempstead HP2 4HW
Record Attendance: 2,254 (vs Gosport Borough during the 2013/14 season)
Pitch Size: 112 × 72 yards

Colours: Shirts and Shorts are Red with White trim
Telephone Nº: (01442) 251521
Fax Number: (01442) 264322
Ground Capacity: 3,152
Seating Capacity: 300
Web site: www.hemelfc.com
E-mail: info@hemelfc.com

GENERAL INFORMATION

Car Parking: At the ground
Coach Parking: At the ground
Nearest Railway Station: Hemel Hempstead (1½ miles)
Nearest Bus Station: Hemel Hempstead (¾ mile)
Club Shop: At the ground (Matchdays only)

GROUND INFORMATION

Away Supporters' Entrances & Sections:
No usual segregation

ADMISSION INFO (2017/2018 PRICES)

Adult Standing: £12.00   **Adult Seating**: £12.00
Concessionary Standing/Seating: £8.00
Under-18s Standing/Seating: £1.00
Under-5s Standing/Seating: Free of charge
Please contact the club for 2018/2019 pricing information.
Programme Price: £2.50

DISABLED INFORMATION

Wheelchairs: Accommodated
Helpers: Admitted
Prices: Normal prices apply
Disabled Toilets: Available in the Clubhouse
Contact: (01442) 259777

Travelling Supporters' Information:
Routes: Exit the M1 at Junction 8 and go straight ahead at the first roundabout. When approaching the 2nd roundabout move into the right hand lane and, as you continue straight across be ready to turn right almost immediately through a gap in the central reservation. This turn-off is Leverstock Green Road and continue along this to the double mini-roundabout. At this roundabout turn left into Vauxhall Road and the ground is on the right at the next roundabout.

HUNGERFORD TOWN FC

Founded: 1886
Former Names: Hungerford Swifts FC
Nickname: 'The Crusaders'
Ground: Town Ground, Bulpit Lane, Hungerford, RG17 0AY
Record Attendance: 1,684 (1988/89 season)

Colours: White shirts with Black shorts
Contact Telephone Nº: (01488) 682939
Ground Capacity: 2,500
Seating Capacity: 250
Web: www.hungerfordtown.com

GENERAL INFORMATION

Car Parking: At the ground and at the local school
Coach Parking: At the ground
Nearest Railway Station: Hungerford (½ mile)
Club Shop: At the ground
Opening Times: Matchdays only
Telephone Nº: (01488) 682939

GROUND INFORMATION

Away Supporters' Entrances & Sections:
No usual segregation

ADMISSION INFO (2018/2019 PRICES)

Adult Standing: £12.00
Adult Seating: £12.00
Concessionary Standing: £6.00
Concessionary Seating: £6.00
Note: Under-16s are admitted free of charge
Programme Price: £2.00

DISABLED INFORMATION

Wheelchairs: Accommodated
Helpers: Admitted
Prices: £6.00 for the disabled. Free of charge for helpers
Disabled Toilets: Available
Contact: (01488) 682939   (Bookings are not necessary)

Travelling Supporters' Information:
Routes: Exit the M4 at Junction 14 and take the A338 towards Hungerford. Upon reaching Hungerford, turn right at the roundabout onto the A4 Bath Road, turn left at the next roundabout into Charnham Street then turn left again into Bridge Street (A338). The road becomes the High Street and pass under the railway line, carry straight on over three mini-roundabouts then take the next left into Priory Road. Continue to the end of the street and continue left into Priory Road then take the 3rd turning on the left into Bulpit Lane. The entrance to the ground is on the left shortly after crossing the junction with Priory Avenue.

OXFORD CITY FC

Founded: 1882
Former Names: None
Nickname: 'City'
Ground: The Oxford City Community Arena, Marsh Lane, Marston, Oxford OX3 0NQ
Record Attendance: 9,500 (vs Leytonstone, 1950)

Colours: Blue & White hooped shirts with Blue shorts
Telephone Nº: (01865) 744493 or 07880 198246
Ground Capacity: 3,218
Seating Capacity: 520
Web Site: www.oxfordcityfc.co.uk
E-mail: ctoxford@btinternet.com

GENERAL INFORMATION
Car Parking: At the ground
Coach Parking: At the ground
Nearest Railway Station: Oxford (3¾ miles)
Club Shop: At the ground
Opening Times: Matchdays only
Telephone Nº: (01865) 744493

GROUND INFORMATION
Away Supporters' Entrances & Sections:
No usual segregation

ADMISSION INFO (2018/2019 PRICES)
Adult Standing: £12.00
Adult Seating: £12.00
Concessionary/Student Standing: £6.00
Concessionary/Student Seating: £6.00
Under-16s Standing: Free of charge
Under-16s Seating: Free of charge

DISABLED INFORMATION
Wheelchairs: Accommodated
Helpers: Admitted
Prices: Normal prices apply for the disabled and helpers
Disabled Toilets: Available
Contact: (01865) 744493 (Bookings are not necessary)

Travelling Supporters' Information:
Routes: The stadium is located by the side of the A40 Northern Bypass Road next to the Marston flyover junction to the north east of Oxford. Exit the A40 at the Marston junction and head into Marsh Lane (B4150). Take the first turn on the left into the OXSRAD Complex then turn immediately left again to follow the approach road to the stadium in the far corner of the site.

SLOUGH TOWN FC

Unfortunately, no photograph of Arbour Park was available at the time of going to press.

Founded: 1890
Former Names: Slough FC and Slough United FC
Nickname: 'The Rebels'
Ground: Arbour Park, Stoke Road, Slough SL2 5AY
Record Attendance: 8,000
Colours: Amber shirts with Navy Blue shorts

Contact Telephone Nº: 07792 126124
Ground Capacity: 2,000
Seating Capacity: 300
Web site: www.sloughtownfc.net

GENERAL INFORMATION
Car Parking: At the ground and other nearby car parks
Coach Parking: At the ground
Nearest Railway Station: Slough (¾ mile)
Nearest Bus Station: Slough (¾ mile)
Club Shop: None

GROUND INFORMATION
Away Supporters' Entrances & Sections:
No usual segregation

ADMISSION INFO (2018/2019 PRICES)
Adult Standing/Seating: £13.00
Senior Citizen Standing/Seating: £9.00
Student Standing/Seating: £5.00
Under-16s Standing/Seating: £3.00 (Under-5s free)
Note: Under-12s must be accompanied by an adult.
Programme Price: £1.50

DISABLED INFORMATION
Wheelchairs: Accommodated
Helpers: Admitted. A free carers pass is available.
Download the relevant form from the club's web site.
Prices: Normal prices apply for the disabled and helpers
Disabled Toilets: Available
Contact: 07792 126124 (Bookings are not necessary)

Travelling Supporters' Information:
Routes: From the South: Exit the M4 at Junction 5 and head west on the A4 (London Road) for approximately 2¾ miles. Pass the Tesco Extra store and the turning to Slough Railway station on your right then turn right onto Stoke Road (B416). Continue along Stoke Road for ¾ mile then Arbour Park is on the right; From the North: Exit the M40 at Junction 2 and head south on the A355 towards Slough. After approximately 1½ miles, turn left onto Parish Lane by the Indian Courtyard and at the end of the road, turn right onto Windsor Road (B416). After 2 miles take the second exit at the roundabout, continuing on the B416 and Arbour Park is on the left after approximately 1 mile.

ST. ALBANS CITY FC

Founded: 1908
Former Names: None
Nickname: 'The Saints'
Ground: Clarence Park, York Road, St. Albans, Hertfordshire   AL1 4PL
Record Attendance: 9,757 (27th February 1926)
Pitch Size: 110 × 80 yards

Colours: Blue shirts with Yellow trim, Blue shorts
Telephone Nº: (01727) 848914
Fax Number: (01727) 848914
Ground Capacity: 5,007
Seating Capacity: 667
Web site: www.stalbanscityfc.com
E-mail: info@stalbanscityfc.com

GENERAL INFORMATION

Car Parking: Street parking or in the railway station car park
Coach Parking: In Clarence Park
Nearest Railway Station: St. Albans City (200 yds)
Club Shop: At the ground
Opening Times: Matchdays only
Telephone Nº: (01727) 864296

GROUND INFORMATION

Away Supporters' Entrances & Sections:
Hatfield Road End when matches are segregated

ADMISSION INFO (2018/2019 PRICES)

Adult Standing/Seating: £15.00
Concessionary Standing/Seating: £10.00
Under-16s Standing/Seating: £5.00
Note: Under-12s are admitted free of charge when accompanied by a paying adult
Programme Price: £2.50

DISABLED INFORMATION

Wheelchairs: Accommodated
Helpers: One admitted per disabled supporter
Prices: Free for disabled, concessionary prices for helpers
Disabled Toilets: Available in the York Road End
Contact: (01727) 864296   (Bookings are not necessary)

Travelling Supporters' Information:
Routes: Take the M1 or M10 to the A405 North Orbital Road and at the roundabout at the start of the M10, go north on the A5183 (Watling Street). Turn right along St. Stephen's Hill and carry along into St. Albans. Continue up Holywell Hill, go through two sets of traffic lights and at the end of St. Peter's Street, take a right turn at the roundabout into Hatfield Road. Follow over the mini-roundabouts and at the second set of traffic lights turn left into Clarence Road and the ground is on the left. Park in Clarence Road and enter the ground via the Park or in York Road and use the entrance by the footbridge.

TORQUAY UNITED FC

Founded: 1899
Former Name: Torquay Town FC (1899-1910)
Nickname: 'Gulls'
Ground: Plainmoor Ground, Torquay   TQ1 3PS
Ground Capacity: 6,200 **Seating Capacity**: 2,841
Record Attendance: 21,908 (29th January 1955)
Pitch Size: 112 × 72 yards

Colours: Yellow shirts and Blue shorts
Telephone Nº: (01803) 328666
Ticket Office: (01803) 328666
Fax Number: (01803) 323976
Web Site: www.torquayunited.com
E-mail: reception@torquayunited.com

GENERAL INFORMATION
Car Parking: Street parking
Coach Parking: Lymington Road Coach Station (½ mile)
Nearest Railway Station: Torquay (2 miles)
Nearest Bus Station: Lymington Road (½ mile)
Club Shop: At the ground
Opening Times: Matchdays and during Office Hours
Telephone Nº: (01803) 328666

GROUND INFORMATION
Away Supporters' Entrances & Sections:
Bristol Street Motors Terrace

ADMISSION INFO (2018/2019 PRICES)
Adult Standing: £13.00
Adult Seating: £14.00 – £15.00
Concessionary Standing/Seating: £11.00
Under-18s Standing/Seating: £7.00
Note: Under-7s are admitted free with a paying adult and Family tickets are also available.
Programme Price: £3.00

DISABLED INFORMATION
Wheelchairs: 9 spaces in front of Bristow Bench Stand for home supporters plus 9 spaces in the Away end.
Helpers: One helper admitted per wheelchair
Prices: Normal prices for the disabled. Free for helpers
Disabled Toilets: Available in the Ellacombe End and the Away End
Contact: (01803) 328666   (Bookings are not necessary)

Travelling Supporters' Information:
Routes: From the North and East: Take the M5 to the A38 then A380 to Torquay. On entering Torquay, turn left at the 1st set of traffic lights after Riviera Way Retail Park into Hele Road. Following signs for the ground, continue straight on over two mini-roundabouts, go up West Hill Road to the traffic lights, then straight ahead into Warbro Road. The ground is situated on the right after 200 yards.

TRURO CITY FC

Late News. Due to circumstances beyond the control of the club, Truro City will be groundsharing with Torquay United for the 2018/19 season.

Founded: 1889
Former Names: None
Nickname: 'White Tigers'
Ground: Treyew Road, Truro   TR1 2TH
Record Attendance: 2,637 (31st March 2007)
Colours: All White shirts and shorts

Telephone Nº: (01872) 225400
Fax Number: (01872) 225402
Ground Capacity: 3,200
Seating Capacity: 1,675
Web Site: www.trurocityfc.net

GENERAL INFORMATION
Car Parking: At the ground
Coach Parking: At the ground
Nearest Railway Station: Truro (½ mile)
Club Shop: None

GROUND INFORMATION
Away Supporters' Entrances & Sections:
No usual segregation

ADMISSION INFO (2018/2019 PRICES)
Adult Standing: £13.00
Adult Seating: £13.00
Concessionary Standing: £11.00
Concessionary Seating: £11.00
Under-18s and Students Standing: £7.00
Under-18s and Students Seating: £7.00
Note: Under-7s are admitted free with a paying adult

DISABLED INFORMATION
Wheelchairs: Accommodated
Helpers: Admitted
Prices: Normal prices apply for the disabled and helpers
Disabled Toilets: Available
Contact: (01872) 225400   (Bookings are not necessary)

Travelling Supporters' Information:
Routes: From the North or East: Take the A30 to the A390 (from the North) or travel straight on the A390 (from the East) to Truro. Continue on the A390 and pass through Truro. The ground is located just to the South West of Truro on the left hand side of the A390 just before the County Hall; From the West: Take the A390 to Truro. The ground is on the right hand side of the road shortly after crossing the railway line and passing the County Hall; From the South: Take the A39 to Truro. At the junction with the A390 turn left onto Green Lane and the ground is on the left hand side of the road after approximately ½ mile.

WEALDSTONE FC

Photo courtesy of Steve Foster/Wealdstone FC

Founded: 1899
Former Names: None
Nickname: 'The Stones' or 'The Royals'
Ground: Grosvenor Vale, Ruislip   HA4 6JQ
Record Attendance: 2,469 (vs Colchester Utd, 2015)
Colours: Royal Blue shirts with White shorts

Telephone N°: 07790 038095
Fax Number: (020) 8930-7143
Ground Capacity: 3,432
Seating Capacity: 698
Web site: www.wealdstone-fc.com
E-mail: clubsecretary@wealdstone-fc.com

GENERAL INFORMATION
Car Parking: 100 spaces available at the ground
Coach Parking: Available outside the ground
Nearest Mainline Station: West Ruislip (1 mile)
Nearest Tube Station: Ruislip (½ mile)
Club Shop: Yes
Opening Times: Orders through the post only
Telephone N°: –

GROUND INFORMATION
Away Supporters' Entrances & Sections:
No usual segregation

ADMISSION INFO (2018/2019 PRICES)
Adult Standing/Seating: £15.00
Concessionary Standing/Seating: £10.00
Under-18s Standing/Seating: £5.00
Note: Under-14s are admitted free of charge when
accompanied by a paying adult
Programme Price: £3.00

DISABLED INFORMATION
Wheelchairs: Accommodated
Helpers: Admitted
Prices: Normal prices apply
Disabled Toilets: Available
Contact: (01895) 637487

Travelling Supporters' Information:
Routes: Exit the M25 at Junction 16 and take the A40 towards Uxbridge. At the Polish War Memorial Junction with the A4180, follow the Ruislip signs (West End Road). After about 1½ miles, turn right into Grosvenor Vale for the ground.

WELLING UNITED FC

Founded: 1963
Former Names: None
Nickname: 'The Wings'
Ground: Park View Road Ground, Welling, Kent, DA16 1SY
Record Attendance: 4,100 (vs Gillingham, 1989)
Pitch Size: 112 × 72 yards

Colours: Shirts are Red with White facings, Red shorts
Telephone Nº: (0208) 301-1196
Daytime Phone Nº: (0208) 301-1196
Fax Number: (0208) 301-5676
Ground Capacity: 4,000
Seating Capacity: 1,000
Web site: www.wellingunited.com
E-mail: info@wellingunited.com

GENERAL INFORMATION

Car Parking: Street parking only
Coach Parking: Outside of the ground
Nearest Railway Station: Welling (¾ mile)
Nearest Bus Station: Bexleyheath
Club Shop: At the ground
Opening Times: Matchdays only
Telephone Nº: (0208) 301-1196

GROUND INFORMATION

Away Supporters' Entrances & Sections:
Accommodation in the Danson Park End

ADMISSION INFO (2018/2019 PRICES)

Adult Standing: £12.00   **Adult Seating**: £14.00
Concessionary Standing: £8.00
Concessionary Seating: £10.00
Under-12s Standing: Free with a paying adult
Under-12s Seating: £2.00 with a paying adult
Programme Price: £3.00

DISABLED INFORMATION

Wheelchairs: Accommodated at the side of the Main Stand
Helpers: Admitted
Prices: Concessionary prices for fans with disabilities.
Helpers are admitted free of charge
Disabled Toilets: Yes
Contact: (0208) 301-1196   (Bookings are not necessary)

Travelling Supporters' Information:
Routes: Take the A2 (Rochester Way) from London, then the A221 Northwards (Danson Road) to Bexleyheath. At the end turn left towards Welling along Park View Road and the ground is on the left.

WESTON-SUPER-MARE FC

Founded: 1899
Former Names: Christ Church Old Boys FC
Nickname: 'Seagulls'
Ground: Woodspring Stadium, Winterstoke Road, Weston-super-Mare   BS24 9AA
Record Attendance: 2,949 (vs Doncaster Rov., 2014)
Pitch Size: 110 × 70 yards

Colours: White shirts with Black shorts
Telephone Nº: (01934) 621618
Fax Number: (01934) 622704
Ground Capacity: 3,500
Seating Capacity: 500
Web site: www.westonsmareafc.co.uk
E-mail: enquiries@wsmafc.co.uk

GENERAL INFORMATION

Car Parking: 140 spaces available at the ground
Coach Parking: At the ground
Nearest Railway Station: Weston-super-Mare (1½ miles)
Nearest Bus Station: Weston-super-Mare (1½ miles)
Club Shop: At the ground
Opening Times: Matchdays only
Telephone Nº: (01934) 621618

GROUND INFORMATION

Away Supporters' Entrances & Sections:
No usual segregation

ADMISSION INFO (2017/2018 PRICES)

Adult Standing/Seating: £12.00
Concessionary Standing/Seating: £8.00
Students and Under-16s Standing/Seating: £3.00
Note: Under-8s are admitted free of charge when accompanied by a paying adult or senior citizen.
Please contact the club for 2018/2019 pricing information.

DISABLED INFORMATION

Wheelchairs: Accommodated in a special disabled section
Helpers: Admitted
Prices: Normal prices apply
Disabled Toilets: Two available
Contact: (01934) 621618   (Bookings are not necessary)

Travelling Supporters' Information:
Routes: Exit the M5 at Junction 21 and follow the dual carriageway (A370) to the 4th roundabout (Asda Winterstoke). Turn left, go over the mini-roundabout and continue for 800 yards. The ground is on the right.

WOKING FC

Founded: 1889
Former Names: None
Nickname: 'Cardinals'
Ground: Laithwaite Community Stadium, Kingfield, Woking, Surrey GU22 9AA
Record Attendance: 6,064 (vs Coventry City, 1997)
Pitch Size: 109 × 76 yards

Colours: Shirts are Red & White halves, Black shorts
Telephone Nº: (01483) 772470
Daytime Phone Nº: (01483) 772470
Fax Number: (01483) 888423
Ground Capacity: 6,161
Seating Capacity: 2,511
Web site: www.wokingfc.co.uk
E-mail: admin@wokingfc.co.uk

GENERAL INFORMATION

Car Parking: Limited parking at the ground
Coach Parking: Please contact the club for details
Nearest Railway Station: Woking (1 mile)
Nearest Bus Station: Woking
Club Shop: At the ground
Opening Times: Weekdays 10.00am to 3.00pm and Matchdays 1.00pm to 3.00pm.
Telephone Nº: (01483) 772470

GROUND INFORMATION

Away Supporters' Entrances & Sections:
Kingfield Road entrance for the Tennis Club terrace

ADMISSION INFO (2018/2019 PRICES)

Adult Standing: £18.00
Adult Seating: £18.00
Under-16s/Student Standing: £5.00
Under-16s/Student Seating: £5.00
Senior Citizen Standing: £13.00
Senior Citizen Seating: £13.00

DISABLED INFORMATION

Wheelchairs: 8 spaces in the Leslie Gosden Stand and 8 spaces in front of the Family Stand
Helpers: Admitted
Prices: One wheelchair and helper for £13.00
Disabled Toilets: Yes – in the Leslie Gosden Stand and Family Stand area
Contact: (01483) 772470 (Bookings are necessary)

Travelling Supporters' Information:
Routes: Exit the M25 at Junction 10 and follow the A3 towards Guildford. Leave at the next junction onto the B2215 through Ripley and join the A247 to Woking. Alternatively, exit the M25 at Junction 11 and follow the A320 to Woking Town Centre. The ground is on the outskirts of Woking – follow signs on the A320 and A247.

National League

2017/2018 Season

	AFC Fylde	Aldershot Town	Barrow	Boreham Wood	Bromley	Chester	Dagenham & Redbridge	Dover Athletic	Eastleigh	Ebbsfleet United	Gateshead	Guiseley	FC Halifax Town	Hartlepool United	Leyton Orient	Macclesfield Town	Maidenhead United	Maidstone United	Solihull Moors	Sutton United	Torquay United	Tranmere Rovers	Woking	Wrexham
AFC Fylde		7-1	1-0	2-2	2-2	1-1	2-2	3-1	2-2	1-1	0-0	2-1	2-0	3-3	0-1	6-0	1-4	3-0	1-1	2-1	2-0	5-2	1-2	2-0
Aldershot Town	2-1		1-1	2-0	1-1	1-2	1-1	0-2	0-2	0-0	1-0	6-0	0-1	2-1	2-2	1-2	1-0	1-1	1-0	2-2	3-2	2-1	3-1	2-0
Barrow	1-3	3-1		2-1	0-3	1-2	0-1	0-0	3-2	0-1	1-1	0-0	0-0	1-2	2-2	0-2	1-1	0-1	1-2	1-1	1-1	1-1	3-0	1-1
Boreham Wood	1-0	2-1	0-0		2-2	4-2	1-2	2-3	1-0	0-1	2-1	3-1	1-1	0-0	2-0	0-2	1-1	1-0	4-1	0-4	2-0	2-1	2-1	0-1
Bromley	0-1	0-2	0-0	3-2		1-1	3-1	2-2	0-0	4-2	0-2	2-1	3-0	2-0	6-1	1-1	2-3	2-2	1-0	0-1	3-1	0-1	2-0	1-1
Chester	1-1	0-0	3-2	1-2	3-2		0-4	2-3	3-1	1-1	1-3	0-2	0-0	1-1	0-1	0-2	2-0	1-3	1-0	2-3	0-2	0-2	0-2	0-1
Dagenham & Redbridge	2-0	0-2	2-1	2-3	5-1	3-2		1-0	1-2	3-3	3-1	3-2	3-1	4-2	0-0	1-0	1-0	2-1	1-3	1-2	1-0	0-4	1-1	0-1
Dover Athletic	0-1	1-2	1-1	0-1	1-2	4-0	1-0		2-0	1-1	3-2	2-1	0-0	4-0	1-0	2-0	1-1	2-2	1-0	0-1	1-0	0-1	3-1	1-0
Eastleigh	2-2	0-0	0-2	0-2	4-4	2-2	2-2	2-1		0-1	3-2	4-2	0-0	4-3	0-0	2-2	0-1		1-2	1-0	1-1	2-0	2-2	1-1
Ebbsfleet United	3-3	0-2	3-2	0-3	2-1	0-1	1-1	2-1	2-2		0-0	4-0	2-0	3-0	2-1	2-2	1-1	0-0	0-1	0-1	0-0	2-1	2-1	3-0
Gateshead	1-2	0-1	1-2	1-1	1-2	3-2	0-0	0-0	2-0	2-5		1-0	0-0	2-2	1-3	3-0	7-1	2-1	2-2	0-2	3-0	1-0	1-1	0-0
Guiseley	1-0	1-1	0-1	0-0	0-1	1-1	3-5	1-1	0-0	2-2	0-1		1-1	0-1	1-3	1-2	1-3	0-0	4-2	0-2	3-2	0-0	1-2	0-2
FC Halifax Town	2-1	0-1	0-1	2-1	4-0	2-1	3-3	1-2	2-2	2-0	2-0	2-0		2-0	1-2	1-4	3-2	0-2	0-0	2-1	1-1	0-2	0-0	1-1
Hartlepool United	0-2	0-2	1-0	0-0	2-1	1-1	1-0	0-1	1-2	0-1	2-2	0-1	4-0		1-0	1-2	1-2	3-1	0-1	1-1	1-1	1-1	3-2	0-2
Leyton Orient	1-2	2-3	4-1	0-0	0-1	2-2	2-0	1-1	1-1	1-1	0-2	4-1	0-3	1-2		0-1		2-0	2-3	4-1		1-1	3-0	1-0
Macclesfield Town	2-1	2-0	3-1	0-0	1-0	2-0	1-0	1-2	1-0	1-0	2-1	2-1	1-1	1-1			1-0	1-4	0-0	1-0	1-1	2-2	1-3	4-1
Maidenhead United	1-2	3-3	0-1	2-1	5-2	3-0	1-1	3-2	3-1	1-1	0-3	3-0	0-0	2-1	0-1	1-1		1-0	1-2	1-0	2-1	1-0	2-1	1-2
Maidstone United	1-0	1-1	0-1	0-4	0-2	1-0	0-0	2-2	2-3	1-2	2-2	1-1	0-0	1-2	0-2	2-2	1-1		1-1	1-0	1-0	2-3	3-1	2-1
Solihull Moors	0-4	0-0	3-3	0-0	2-0	2-0	2-2	3-2	1-4	1-3	1-1	3-1	1-2	1-0	0-1	3-1	1-0			0-2	1-1	0-2	3-0	0-0
Sutton United	2-1	2-1	3-2	1-1	0-3	3-2	2-1	2-2	2-0	0-0	1-1	4-0	3-2	1-1	2-0	0-2	0-2	1-3	1-0		0-1	1-3	2-0	1-1
Torquay United	1-3	0-0	3-1	2-4	0-4	1-1	0-3	0-2	1-2	1-1	1-1	3-4	1-0	0-2	3-0	0-1	4-0	0-1	1-2	2-3		0-0	2-1	0-0
Tranmere Rovers	4-1	2-0	1-0	2-2	1-0	0-0	2-0	0-1	3-1	3-0	4-2	4-0	4-2	1-2	2-1	1-4	3-2	4-0	1-2	0-1	3-0		3-1	0-1
Woking	1-0	1-2	1-2	0-0	0-2	1-0	1-0	1-2	2-1	1-0	2-1	2-3	1-3	1-1	0-2	2-3	1-1	1-0	1-1	2-1	2-0	0-1		2-2
Wrexham	0-0	2-2	3-3	0-1	2-0	2-0	1-2	0-0	2-1	2-0	1-0	1-1	1-1	0-0	2-2	0-1	2-0	1-0	1-0	1-1	4-0	2-2	1-0	

National League

Season 2017/2018

	P	W	D	L	F	A	Pts
Macclesfield Town	46	27	11	8	67	46	92
Tranmere Rovers	46	24	10	12	78	46	82
Sutton United	46	23	10	13	67	53	79
Boreham Wood	46	20	15	11	64	47	75
Aldershot Town	46	20	15	11	64	52	75
Ebbsfleet United	46	19	17	10	64	50	74
AFC Fylde	46	20	13	13	82	56	73
Dover Athletic	46	20	13	13	62	44	73
Bromley	46	19	13	14	75	58	70
Wrexham	46	17	19	10	49	39	70
Dagenham & Redbridge	46	19	11	16	69	62	68
Maidenhead United	46	17	13	16	65	66	64
Leyton Orient	46	16	12	18	58	56	60
Eastleigh	46	13	17	16	65	72	56
Hartlepool United	46	14	14	18	53	63	56
FC Halifax Town	46	13	16	17	48	58	55
Gateshead	46	12	18	16	62	58	54
Solihull Moors	46	14	12	20	49	60	54
Maidstone United	46	13	15	18	52	64	54
Barrow	46	11	16	19	51	63	49
Woking	46	13	9	24	55	76	48
Torquay United	46	10	12	24	45	73	42
Chester	46	8	13	25	42	79	37
Guiseley	46	7	12	27	44	89	33

National League Promotion Play-offs

Aldershot Town 1   Ebbsfleet United .... 1 (aet)
Ebbsfleet United won 5-4 on penalties
Boreham Wood 2   AFC Fylde 1

Tranmere Rovers 4   Ebbsfleet United .... 2 (aet)
Sutton United 2   Boreham Wood 3

Tranmere Rovers 2   Boreham Wood 1

Promoted: Macclesfield Town and Tranmere Rovers

Relegated: Woking, Torquay United, Chester and Guiseley

National League North — 2017/2018 Season

	AFC Telford United	Alfreton Town	Blyth Spartans	Boston United	Brackley Town	Bradford Park Avenue	Chorley	Curzon Ashton	Darlington	FC United of Manchester	Gainsborough Trinity	Harrogate Town	Kidderminster Harriers	Leamington	North Ferriby United	Nuneaton Town	Salford City	Southport	Spennymoor Town	Stockport County	Tamworth	York City
AFC Telford United		1-2	2-3	2-1	1-3	1-4	1-2	0-3	0-0	1-0	3-2	1-5	0-0	3-2	3-0	1-2	0-2	1-1	3-2	3-2	2-0	3-5
Alfreton Town	0-1		2-0	2-3	1-1	1-3	0-2	4-0	1-1	1-0	4-1	1-2	0-2	4-1	1-0	1-1	2-3	0-1	1-4	1-3	2-1	2-3
Blyth Spartans	0-1	0-1		5-2	3-0	3-0	2-0	2-1	3-1	1-1	4-0	0-2	1-2	1-0	0-1	6-3	0-1	2-0	2-3	0-1	4-2	0-2
Boston United	1-0	3-1	2-1		2-3	1-2	2-0	3-3	1-1	4-4	2-0	3-0	3-2	0-1	2-1	1-1	0-1	3-2	0-3	2-2	3-1	2-1
Brackley Town	1-1	1-3	3-1	4-1		0-1	1-2	2-2	3-0	2-1	2-0	0-0	2-0	1-1	3-0	1-0	2-1	4-0	2-0	3-2	0-0	2-0
Bradford Park Avenue	2-1	3-3	4-1	2-1	2-0		0-0	3-1	0-1	3-0	5-0	3-1	1-1	1-0	0-1	1-1	1-2	1-2	1-2	2-3	3-4	0-5
Chorley	3-2	1-0	2-0	0-1	0-0	2-0		1-1	4-1	1-0	1-0	0-1	0-0	2-0	2-2	2-2	0-1	0-0	3-1	1-1	1-1	2-0
Curzon Ashton	1-0	2-2	0-3	2-1	0-2	1-1	0-2		1-0	1-0	2-0	1-2	1-2	1-1	4-0	2-2	1-1	2-2	1-0	1-1	1-0	4-1
Darlington	0-1	4-1	3-0	1-2	0-3	2-1	2-2	1-0		3-0	4-3	3-1	2-1	0-0	6-0	0-0	1-2	2-4	1-1	1-1	0-1	1-2
FC United of Manchester	3-1	3-2	1-3	2-1	1-1	4-0	0-0	2-0	1-2		1-0	3-2	1-2	1-2	0-2	2-1	3-2	1-0	2-3	0-1	3-1	1-0
Gainsborough Trinity	3-2	2-1	2-4	1-1	1-2	0-3	1-0	1-0	3-1	1-0		4-5	1-0	1-2	2-0	0-1	0-3	4-1	2-3	3-0	1-0	
Harrogate Town	2-1	4-3	5-1	3-1	1-1	1-1	4-1	5-0	3-0	6-0	2-0		2-2	2-2	3-0	4-0	1-2	2-0	1-2	4-1	3-0	2-0
Kidderminster Harriers	2-0	2-1	5-4	1-1	2-1	1-2	0-1	2-2	3-3	4-0	3-0	0-2		2-0	4-0	3-0	4-4	3-0	2-2	3-1	2-0	2-1
Leamington	0-3	2-3	1-0	0-2	2-2	2-1	2-0	0-0	2-3	1-0	3-0	1-3	1-1		3-0	1-0	0-4	0-1	4-0	2-3	1-2	2-2
North Ferriby United	0-2	0-3	1-0	1-5	0-5	0-1	0-2	0-1	1-1	3-3	0-1	0-2	1-3	1-1		0-2	1-1	0-3	0-6	1-3	0-0	1-4
Nuneaton Town	0-2	2-2	2-2	1-1	0-2	0-0	1-1	1-1	2-1	1-0	0-1	2-1	1-0	4-0	2-2		0-2	3-0	0-1	1-3	4-1	1-0
Salford City	3-0	1-0	4-1	1-2	2-0	2-2	0-3	2-1	0-2	2-2	1-0	2-1	3-0	2-3	4-0	3-0		2-1	3-2	2-1	2-1	3-2
Southport	3-0	1-3	0-3	4-0	0-1	0-4	3-0	3-1	2-0	3-3	2-2	1-4	0-3	2-0	2-2	0-1	0-1		1-2	3-1	3-0	1-1
Spennymoor Town	1-2	2-1	3-1	0-0	0-3	3-0	1-0	2-4	1-2	4-4	1-1	3-1	1-1	1-0	1-1	0-1	1-1	2-1		1-0	1-0	2-4
Stockport County	1-0	1-0	1-3	1-0	0-1	0-0	1-1	3-0	1-1	4-1	1-0	2-2	1-2	4-0	4-1	0-1	2-2	6-0	3-2		3-2	2-0
Tamworth	2-2	2-3	0-3	2-1	1-1	0-1	3-4	4-1	0-0	0-2	1-2	1-2	2-1	0-3	4-1	2-0	1-2	3-3	3-1	3-1		1-1
York City	0-1	1-1	2-3	1-0	0-2	2-1	1-1	2-1	0-0	0-2	1-1	0-2	1-1	2-2	2-0	4-3	1-0	3-2	2-2	2-0	2-3	

National League North

Season 2017/2018

	P	W	D	L	F	A	Pts
Salford City	42	28	7	7	80	45	91
Harrogate Town	42	26	7	9	100	49	85
Brackley Town	42	23	11	8	72	37	80
Kidderminster Harriers	42	20	12	10	76	50	72
Stockport County	42	20	9	13	75	57	69
Chorley	42	18	14	10	52	39	68
Bradford Park Avenue	42	18	9	15	66	56	63
Spennymoor Town	42	18	9	15	71	67	63
Boston United	42	17	9	16	67	66	60
Blyth Spartans	42	19	2	21	76	69	59
York City	42	16	10	16	65	62	58
Darlington	42	14	13	15	58	58	55
Nuneaton Town	42	14	13	15	50	57	55
AFC Telford United	42	16	5	21	55	69	53
Southport	42	14	8	20	60	72	50
FC United of Manchester	42	14	8	20	58	72	50
Alfreton Town	42	14	7	21	67	71	49
Curzon Ashton	42	12	13	17	52	66	49
Leamington	42	13	10	19	51	65	49
Gainsborough Trinity	42	14	4	24	47	73	46
Tamworth	42	11	9	22	55	77	42
North Ferriby United	42	4	9	29	25	101	21

National League North Promotion Play-offs

Stockport County .... 0 — Chorley 1
Kidderminster Harriers .... 0 — Bradford Park Avenue 2

Harrogate Town .... 2 — Chorley 1
Brackley Town .... 1 — Bradford Park Avenue 0

Harrogate Town .... 3 — Brackley 0

Promoted: Salford City and Harrogate Town

Relegated: Worcester City, Stalybridge Celtic and Altrincham

National League South
2017/2018 Season

	Bath City	Bognor Regis Town	Braintree Town	Chelmsford City	Chippenham Town	Concord Rangers	Dartford	Eastbourne Borough	East Thurrock United	Gloucester City	Hampton & Richmond Borough	Havant & Waterlooville	Hemel Hempstead Town	Hungerford Town	Oxford City	Poole Town	St Albans City	Truro City	Wealdstone	Welling United	Weston-super-Mare	Whitehawk
Bath City	■	0-0	1-1	1-2	2-5	2-0	1-2	0-1	4-0	5-1	2-0	1-2	0-0	5-0	2-1	1-0	2-1	0-0	0-0	1-1	0-2	1-1
Bognor Regis Town	3-2	■	2-1	0-1	1-3	1-2	1-2	0-1	0-2	2-2	1-2	0-3	2-3	1-2	0-0	1-1	2-1	0-2	0-3	1-3	1-1	6-2
Braintree Town	0-2	3-0	■	2-2	2-0	2-1	2-2	3-2	4-0	3-0	2-1	1-3	1-2	5-0	0-0	1-0	1-0	1-1	2-2	1-1	0-1	4-3
Chelmsford City	1-1	0-0	2-2	■	2-0	1-0	1-0	5-2	1-2	2-0	1-2	0-2	3-3	1-1	1-2	2-1	0-2	2-0	3-0	4-1	1-1	4-2
Chippenham Town	0-3	1-0	1-1	3-2	■	1-2	2-2	4-0	2-2	2-0	3-3	0-0	5-1	1-2	3-2	0-1	3-3	2-0	0-0	1-0	2-0	2-1
Concord Rangers	0-1	2-1	0-1	0-2	4-2	■	1-1	2-1	1-4	1-1	1-0	1-1	1-0	1-0	2-1	0-1	1-2	2-2	3-1	0-2	2-2	1-0
Dartford	2-0	3-1	1-1	1-2	3-0	2-0	■	4-2	0-1	4-1	1-0	1-0	3-2	0-0	7-1	0-1	2-1	4-1	3-3	4-1	3-1	3-1
Eastbourne Borough	2-3	3-0	2-3	0-3	4-2	3-1	0-1	■	2-2	0-1	1-2	1-4	0-2	4-1	2-0	0-4	1-1	1-3	1-1	0-0	1-2	1-4
East Thurrock United	1-1	2-0	5-3	2-4	0-2	2-3	0-1	0-0	■	3-0	1-1	0-1	0-1	0-1	4-1	2-2	1-1	1-2	1-1	0-1	3-4	4-2
Gloucester City	2-1	3-2	1-3	0-2	1-0	1-0	0-1	1-2	3-1	■	1-1	0-1	1-0	4-0	0-1	2-2	1-4	0-3	2-2	0-1	1-3	3-1
Hampton & Richmond	3-1	1-0	1-1	1-1	1-0	1-1	2-2	1-1	5-1	1-1	■	0-1	0-0	3-1	1-0	1-0	1-0	1-1	1-1	1-1	3-1	1-1
Havant & Waterlooville	1-2	0-0	0-0	1-1	4-0	3-2	0-0	3-2	6-1	2-1	0-0	■	1-1	2-0	3-2	2-2	2-1	1-2	1-0	2-3	2-0	4-0
Hemel Hempstead Town	1-1	3-1	4-3	3-1	3-1	1-1	0-3	3-0	2-0	3-1	1-0	0-0	■	1-2	2-0	0-1	2-0	1-2	1-0	2-2	1-1	3-0
Hungerford Town	1-2	1-1	0-1	1-1	2-1	2-0	1-0	0-1	2-2	2-3	2-2	0-1	0-2	■	1-2	4-0	3-1	0-1	1-3	1-4	2-0	0-1
Oxford City	1-1	4-0	1-2	2-0	0-1	1-1	0-2	2-1	3-3	0-1	0-1	4-1	2-0	1-2	■	2-3	2-3	3-1	3-2	1-1	3-3	0-1
Poole Town	0-4	2-2	0-3	0-0	2-0	1-1	0-1	0-4	2-3	0-3	0-1	1-3	2-4	1-2	2-0	■	0-1	0-3	2-1	2-3	3-1	1-1
St Albans City	2-0	1-2	2-1	2-1	2-0	2-1	4-0	2-2	7-2	2-3	1-3	2-1	2-2	0-0	1-1	2-1	■	0-1	2-1	1-2	3-1	0-3
Truro City	1-2	1-1	1-2	2-0	1-0	0-2	3-1	0-1	1-2	1-1	1-1	1-0	3-3	2-1	2-3	3-1	1-2	■	1-3	3-2	3-1	7-2
Wealdstone	2-1	3-0	3-1	0-2	4-4	2-1	1-2	2-3	3-0	1-2	0-3	0-1	1-1	1-0	1-1	4-1	1-3	2-1	■	1-0	2-1	2-1
Welling United	0-2	3-3	3-0	0-1	4-0	3-3	2-3	3-0	0-3	2-3	0-1	0-1	0-0	3-2	1-3	2-0	3-1	2-2	1-2	■	3-1	1-0
Weston-super-Mare	4-2	1-0	1-2	0-1	2-2	1-0	3-0	5-1	2-2	2-1	1-2	1-4	2-1	2-1	4-2	1-2	0-2	0-2	5-1	0-2	■	1-0
Whitehawk	1-1	2-2	1-1	0-2	1-3	2-0	0-4	0-1	2-3	1-1	1-3	0-0	0-5	0-3	0-3	2-2	1-1	3-2	0-1	2-1	5-1	■

National League South
Season 2017/2018

Havant & Waterlooville	42	25	11	6	70	30	86
Dartford	42	26	8	8	81	44	86
Chelmsford City	42	21	11	10	68	45	74
Hampton & Richmond Borough	42	18	18	6	58	37	72
Hemel Hempstead Town	42	19	13	10	71	51	70
Braintree Town	42	19	13	10	73	55	69
Truro City	42	20	9	13	71	55	69
St. Albans City	42	19	8	15	71	58	65
Bath City	42	17	12	13	64	48	63
Welling United	42	17	10	15	68	59	61
Wealdstone	42	16	11	15	64	62	59
Weston-super-Mare	42	16	7	19	66	73	55
Chippenham Town	42	15	9	18	64	70	54
Gloucester City	42	15	8	19	56	70	53
East Thurrock United	42	13	11	18	68	84	50
Oxford City	42	13	10	19	60	69	49
Concord Rangers	42	12	10	20	46	62	46
Eastbourne Borough	42	13	7	22	57	80	46
Hungerford Town	42	12	7	23	45	68	43
Poole Town	42	11	9	22	47	73	42
Whitehawk	42	8	10	24	51	89	34
Bognor Regis Town	42	5	12	25	41	78	27

Braintree Town had 1 point deducted for fielding an ineligible player.

National League South Promotion Play-offs

Hemel Hempstead Town 0   Braintree Town .... 0 (aet)
Braintree Town won 3-2 on penalties.
Hampton & Richmond Boro .. 3   Truro City .... 1 (aet)

Dartford 0   Braintree Town 1
Chelmsford City 0   Hampton & Richmond Boro ... 1

Hampton & Richmond Boro .. 1   Braintree Town .... 1 (aet)
Braintree Town won 4-3 on penalties.

Promoted: Maidenhead United and Braintree Town

Relegated: Poole Town, Whitehawk and Bognor Regis Town

Northern Premier League Premier Division 2017/2018 Season	Altrincham	Ashton United	Barwell	Buxton	Coalville Town	Farsley Celtic	Grantham Town	Halesowen Town	Hednesford Town	Lancaster City	Marine	Matlock Town	Mickleover Sports	Nantwich Town	Rushall Olympic	Shaw Lane	Stafford Rangers	Stalybridge Celtic	Stourbridge	Sutton Coldfield Town	Warrington Town	Whitby Town	Witton Albion	Workington
Altrincham	■	3-2	4-0	1-1	4-2	6-0	1-0	3-0	3-0	4-0	1-1	3-0	1-1	5-1	4-0	5-1	0-3	1-2	4-1	2-1	1-1	1-0	3-4	2-3
Ashton United	3-3	■	1-1	1-4	1-2	1-1	2-1	3-0	1-2	2-1	3-0	3-0	1-1	2-1	2-1	3-3	1-0	1-2	1-0	2-0	2-0	4-0	2-1	0-1
Barwell	1-3	1-1	■	2-1	2-1	3-4	1-1	1-1	1-1	1-0	0-4	2-1	2-1	0-2	4-4	1-0	1-2	1-0	1-1	2-1	0-1	1-0	0-1	1-0
Buxton	0-0	1-0	1-1	■	2-2	3-3	0-3	2-1	2-2	1-2	2-1	2-3	0-2	3-0	1-2	0-2	1-1	2-2	1-1	0-1	2-1	0-2	2-0	4-2
Coalville Town	0-3	1-2	0-3	1-5	■	2-3	1-3	1-0	5-2	1-4	2-3	2-1	2-0	0-3	2-5	1-3	0-0	4-0	0-1	4-2	0-3	0-1	2-1	3-0
Farsley Celtic	0-1	3-3	1-2	3-0	3-1	■	3-0	3-1	1-3	0-0	3-0	1-2	0-3	2-0	1-0	4-2	1-0	5-4	1-4	0-1	0-2	4-0	1-1	3-3
Grantham Town	0-2	1-1	4-1	0-1	0-1	2-2	■	1-2	1-1	3-2	5-0	2-1	0-3	0-0	7-1	3-1	1-2	0-0	4-2	6-1	0-0	2-0	1-1	3-2
Halesowen Town	0-2	1-1	1-0	1-3	2-3	1-2	1-3	■	2-1	4-3	1-1	3-2	0-0	0-1	2-0	0-0	2-0	1-1	1-1	2-0	1-1	3-1	1-3	1-5
Hednesford Town	0-3	1-1	2-3	1-2	1-1	2-1	1-3	2-0	■	1-1	3-2	2-0	1-3	1-0	1-1	1-3	2-1	2-1	1-1	3-0	0-2	0-0	1-0	1-1
Lancaster City	1-2	0-3	1-1	1-1	4-2	1-1	3-1	2-0	0-1	■	3-0	1-2	1-1	1-2	0-2	2-0	1-1	1-0	0-0	1-1	2-2	4-1	4-0	2-2
Marine	0-3	3-4	0-1	2-3	0-1	1-2	1-1	1-0	2-0	3-0	■	1-2	1-3	1-1	2-2	1-1	3-1	0-4	5-0	0-4	0-3	2-2		
Matlock Town	1-0	1-2	0-2	3-3	3-1	1-2	2-3	2-0	3-2	4-3	2-2	■	1-0	0-3	2-1	0-1	2-0	2-0	0-0	5-0	1-3	1-2	2-3	2-0
Mickleover Sports	1-2	2-5	3-3	2-2	2-2	2-2	1-0	0-0	5-0	0-1	1-2	2-0	■	1-2	1-1	1-3	0-2	1-0	1-2	2-0	1-3	2-1	1-1	2-0
Nantwich Town	1-1	2-3	2-2	1-3	1-3	1-1	3-1	1-3	1-5	3-0	1-1	0-2	1-2	■	1-2	2-3	0-3	2-3	2-0	0-0	2-1	1-0	3-2	2-0
Rushall Olympic	2-0	4-2	1-1	2-0	1-1	1-1	0-2	3-1	1-2	3-0	0-2	1-0	1-0	1-4	■	1-3	1-2	1-1	5-1	1-3	3-3	0-0	1-1	
Shaw Lane	1-2	0-0	3-2	2-0	2-0	1-0	0-2	3-2	3-1	0-0	1-3	2-1	1-2	0-2	2-0	■	5-2	2-0	3-1	3-1	5-0	0-0	1-1	3-2
Stafford Rangers	0-2	1-0	1-0	1-4	4-1	0-2	1-2	0-0	0-1	2-2	1-4	2-0	1-1	3-0	0-4	1-2	■	2-0	1-0	4-1	0-0	2-2	0-4	1-2
Stalybridge Celtic	0-0	2-2	4-2	0-1	0-3	1-4	1-3	1-0	2-2	5-2	4-1	0-5	1-0	1-2	1-2	2-0		■	3-1	1-1	2-0	3-1	0-5	1-3
Stourbridge	1-1	2-3	2-1	2-1	1-2	1-2	0-2	1-2	0-0	0-2	1-1	1-1	1-1	5-0	1-1	0-0	4-1		■	2-1	1-1	0-0	1-1	
Sutton Coldfield Town	0-4	0-2	0-6	2-1	1-1	0-1	1-2	0-1	4-1	0-2	3-1	3-3	2-1	1-3	3-4	3-1	2-3	2-0	0-4	■	0-2	1-1	2-6	4-1
Warrington Town	0-0	0-1	2-0	1-0	1-3	4-2	2-1	1-1	4-1	5-1	0-0	2-0	3-1	0-0	2-1	1-0	0-1	1-5	2-1		■	2-1	2-2	1-1
Whitby Town	1-1	3-2	1-0	1-1	2-2	0-2	1-5	5-0	2-2	0-5	3-2	0-3	3-2	2-1	2-3	0-3	0-0	4-1	1-3	2-2	2-2	■	1-2	1-1
Witton Albion	0-2	1-1	2-2	1-0	5-2	1-4	2-3	2-3	3-0	2-0	1-1	3-3	0-2	4-1	1-2	4-0	1-2	4-1	1-0	1-0	1-2	1-0	■	1-0
Workington	5-2	1-2	0-2	1-2	1-0	1-2	0-2	3-1	1-0	2-0	2-1	0-1	3-0	2-1	4-1	2-0	0-0	3-4	2-1	4-0	1-1	1-3	1-1	■

Evo-Stik League – Northern Premier Division

Season 2017/2018

Altrincham	46	28	11	7	101	42	95
Ashton United	46	23	13	10	85	59	82
Warrington Town	46	23	13	10	72	49	82
Grantham Town	46	24	9	13	90	55	81
Farsley Celtic	46	23	11	12	87	69	80
Shaw Lane	46	25	7	14	79	62	79
Witton Albion	46	19	13	14	83	63	70
Rushall Olympic	46	19	9	18	73	79	66
Buxton	46	17	13	16	71	66	64
Barwell	46	17	13	16	65	67	64
Stourbridge	46	16	14	16	67	56	62
Workington	46	18	8	20	72	69	62
Mickleover Sports	46	16	13	17	68	60	61
Stafford Rangers	46	16	13	17	54	58	61
Matlock Town	46	18	6	22	69	75	60
Nantwich Town	46	16	9	21	62	72	57
Hednesford Town	46	15	12	19	60	79	57
Lancaster City	46	14	13	19	66	72	55
Marine	46	14	11	21	67	78	53
Coalville Town	46	15	7	24	70	92	52
Whitby Town	46	12	14	20	60	82	50
Stalybridge Celtic	46	14	6	26	57	90	48
Halesowen Town	46	13	10	23	48	76	45
Sutton Coldfield Town	46	10	6	30	52	108	35

Shaw Lane had 3 points deducted for fielding an ineligible player.
Halesowen Town had 4 points for fielding an ineligible player.
Sutton Coldfield Town had 1 point deducted for fielding an ineligible player.

Promotion Play-offs

Ashton United	2	Farsley Celtic	1
Warrington Town	0	Grantham Town	3
Ashton United	2	Grantham Town	0

Promoted: Altrincham and Ashton United

Relegated: Sutton Coldfield Town

Southern Football League Premier Division 2017/2018 Season	Banbury United	Basingstoke Town	Biggleswade Town	Bishop's Stortford	Chesham United	Dorchester Town	Dunstable Town	Farnborough	Frome Town	Gosport Borough	Hereford	Hitchin Town	Kettering Town	King's Lynn Town	Kings Langley	Merthyr Town	Redditch United	Royston Town	Slough Town	St. Ives Town	St. Neots Town	Stratford Town	Tiverton Town	Weymouth
Banbury United		1-1	1-1	2-1	1-1	5-1	1-2	4-1	3-4	5-0	0-1	1-0	1-1	1-2	1-1	3-3	1-3	3-0	2-2	3-1	1-1	4-0	1-2	1-2
Basingstoke Town	3-1		2-0	3-2	5-0	1-1	2-0	4-3	1-3	3-0	3-1	1-0	3-2	1-2	4-3	2-0	3-0	0-0	1-4	3-2	1-0	2-1	6-2	3-3
Biggleswade Town	1-1	1-2		2-2	0-3	1-1	0-2	3-0	1-2	2-0	0-1	2-1	0-0	2-2	2-0	2-1	1-0	1-1	3-5	0-2	2-0	3-1	4-0	1-2
Bishop's Stortford	0-5	2-0	0-0		1-1	1-0	4-1	2-2	4-0	2-1	0-1	0-3	0-2	2-3	2-0	4-0	3-0	0-3	2-2	4-3	1-2	1-1	1-2	2-3
Chesham United	1-3	4-1	2-0	2-1		2-2	2-0	0-0	5-1	3-0	1-3	0-0	2-0	1-3	1-0	13-1	2-0	1-2	1-1	4-0	2-2	1-3	1-1	0-6
Dorchester Town	0-2	1-0	2-1	1-0	1-1		1-1	4-0	1-4	7-2	0-1	1-4	4-1	0-2	1-0	1-2	1-0	1-0	0-1	6-0	0-4	1-2	3-0	0-3
Dunstable Town	0-5	0-6	0-2	0-5	1-4	0-1		1-0	1-2	0-2	0-4	0-4	1-2	0-4	1-4	0-6	1-1	0-5	0-3	0-2	2-3	2-3	1-2	2-1
Farnborough	1-0	4-3	2-1	0-5	2-0	3-3	4-0		5-3	1-2	2-4	4-1	3-4	5-2	0-4	2-2	1-3	0-1	1-2	2-1	2-4	1-4	2-3	2-6
Frome Town	0-2	1-0	2-3	2-1	1-3	3-1	3-0	1-1		2-0	0-3	3-4	2-2	0-0	2-1	1-2	1-0	1-4	0-4	0-1	2-2	3-0	0-1	1-4
Gosport Borough	0-4	0-8	1-1	1-3	1-5	3-3	1-0	2-4	7-0		0-4	0-3	0-7	1-7	1-2	1-1	2-5	2-3	1-5	0-0	0-1	0-1	0-5	0-4
Hereford	3-0	4-1	1-0	2-0	3-0	4-1	2-0	0-1	1-0	5-1		5-0	4-1	0-2	3-0	1-1	5-2	2-0	0-1	4-0	1-0	5-2	1-0	2-0
Hitchin Town	0-3	2-1	0-1	1-0	0-0	0-0	1-0	1-3	5-1	2-1	0-3		0-0	0-4	6-0	2-0	1-0	0-1		2-2	2-2	4-0	1-2	3-1
Kettering Town	3-0	3-0	3-1	6-0	3-1	4-3	6-0	6-2	3-0	2-0	1-3	4-1		1-0	1-1	5-0	1-0	4-1	0-0	4-1	3-0	2-3	2-0	
King's Lynn Town	1-1	2-1	3-0	2-1	1-0	5-0	3-1	0-0	2-0	3-2	2-0	2-1			3-2	0-0	3-1	4-0	1-0	1-1	1-1		2-0	
Kings Langley	3-4	1-1	1-1	4-1	0-0	2-2	1-0	0-3	2-7	1-1	3-3	1-2	2-5	0-0		2-2	1-2	1-0	0-2	0-3	4-3	2-0	2-2	2-3
Merthyr Town	1-3	1-1	0-2	0-0	1-2	1-1	3-1	3-0	3-4	5-0	0-0	0-0	2-4	0-1	4-1		2-2	2-1	4-5	3-2	1-0	3-1	2-1	0-3
Redditch United	2-2	3-0	1-0	2-2	3-1	4-0	5-0	7-1	4-1	4-2	0-2	2-2	0-0	0-1	2-2	1-1		1-0	1-4	4-0	2-2	0-2	3-2	1-2
Royston Town	1-1	1-0	4-0	4-2	0-2	3-1	1-1	4-3	3-0	5-0	1-4	2-1	4-3	2-0	4-0	5-1	2-1		0-4	2-1	2-1	1-2	3-0	1-2
Slough Town	0-1	1-1	2-1	2-4	2-1	0-2	8-1	5-1	2-1	5-1	2-2	4-0	1-2	2-2	1-1	3-2	4-0	2-1		3-0	2-1	1-1	2-0	3-0
St. Ives Town	2-2	2-2	1-2	0-1	0-2	1-2	2-1	2-4	2-2	1-0	0-2	1-3	3-4	1-3	1-1	2-3	1-0	1-3	1-4		1-1	2-6	1-2	1-2
St. Neots Town	3-0	2-1	0-0	2-2	3-1	5-0	2-2	0-1	1-6	0-4	1-3	1-1	2-4	0-5	3-2	5-2	2-1	3-1	3-1	3-1		2-2	1-0	1-2
Stratford Town	2-3	0-1	1-0	3-1	1-3	2-0	5-1	2-2	1-2	2-0	1-2	0-4	1-5	3-1	2-2	0-0	1-1	0-1	3-0	1-1			1-2	0-0
Tiverton Town	0-0	3-2	3-1	2-1	1-2	0-0	7-1	2-0	2-2	2-0	2-2	3-1	0-3	1-0	3-2	3-1	1-0	1-2	3-0	2-3	1-2	2-1		2-1
Weymouth	1-1	3-2	2-0	1-1	1-0	2-2	2-0	6-0	0-2	5-0	0-2	3-0	3-1	3-1	2-0	3-2	5-0	3-0	1-0	0-1	3-1	1-1	2-0	

Evo-Stik Southern Premier
Premier Division

Season 2017/2018

Team	P	W	D	L	F	A	Pts
Hereford	46	36	5	5	111	33	113
King's Lynn Town	46	30	10	6	99	39	100
Slough Town	46	30	9	7	111	49	99
Kettering Town	46	30	7	9	122	56	97
Weymouth	46	30	7	9	103	48	97
Tiverton Town	46	24	6	16	78	69	78
Royston Town	46	24	5	17	84	65	77
Chesham United	46	21	11	14	85	61	74
Banbury United	46	19	15	12	90	59	72
Basingstoke Town	46	21	8	17	92	72	71
Hitchin Town	46	19	9	18	67	66	66
St. Neots Town	46	17	13	16	79	79	64
Frome Town	46	18	7	21	78	96	61
Redditch United	46	15	10	21	73	73	55
Stratford Town	46	15	10	21	68	81	55
Biggleswade Town	46	14	11	21	52	63	53
Merthyr Town	46	13	14	19	76	98	53
Bishop's Stortford	46	14	10	22	74	79	52
Dorchester Town	46	13	12	21	62	83	51
Farnborough	46	15	6	25	82	120	51
Kings Langley	46	8	14	24	63	98	38
St. Ives Town	46	8	9	29	54	105	33
Gosport Borough	46	5	5	36	41	142	20
Dunstable Town	46	4	5	37	27	137	17

Promotion Play-offs

King's Lynn Town 3   Weymouth 0
Slough Town 3   Kettering Town 1

King's Lynn Town 1   Slough Town 2

Promoted: Hereford and Slough Town

Relegated: Dunstable Town

Isthmian League — Premier Division — 2017/2018 Season

	Billericay Town	Brightlingsea Regent	Burgess Hill Town	Dorking Wanderers	Dulwich Hamlet	Enfield Town	Folkestone Invicta	Harlow Town	Harrow Borough	Hendon	Kingstonian	Leatherhead	Leiston	Lowestoft Town	Margate	Merstham	Metropolitan Police	Needham Market	Staines Town	Thurrock	Tonbridge Angels	Tooting & Mitcham United	Wingate & Finchley	Worthing
Billericay Town		4-0	6-1	1-0	1-3	2-1	2-2	2-0	2-0	4-3	0-1	1-0	4-0	5-0	1-1	2-2	3-0	5-0	5-3	1-0	2-1	1-0	2-2	4-0
Brightlingsea Regent	1-1		5-2	2-3	2-2	2-1	1-2	3-1	1-1	2-1	2-0	0-7	0-1	2-0	0-1	1-3	0-1	2-3	2-2	1-3	0-3	0-3	1-0	3-0
Burgess Hill Town	3-4	1-2		1-3	1-1	2-4	1-1	2-0	2-3	2-4	5-1	0-1	2-1	0-5	1-1	0-0	1-4	1-1	1-1	2-5	0-1	3-1	3-1	4-1
Dorking Wanderers	0-1	3-2	2-1		0-1	2-2	5-3	2-2	0-4	0-3	1-3	1-1	0-2	8-0	4-2	4-0	4-1	3-2	1-1	2-0	2-3	2-2	2-2	4-2
Dulwich Hamlet	1-3	2-1	3-2	4-0		1-1	4-3	4-0	2-0	0-1	4-0	4-0	3-0	1-0	1-1	1-2	0-0	2-0	1-1	2-1	1-2	2-1	1-2	3-0
Enfield Town	1-1	2-0	3-2	3-2	3-1		1-1	1-0	3-0	1-0	1-3	0-1	2-2	3-0	2-1	2-2	4-4	0-2	3-4	3-1	0-1	1-1	1-1	0-1
Folkestone Invicta	2-1	3-2	3-1	3-1	0-3	5-1		1-1	1-3	3-2	3-0	3-0	2-0	1-1	2-1	5-2	0-2	2-0	2-2	3-1	3-1	5-0	1-2	
Harlow Town	2-4	2-0	1-1	2-2	2-3	0-2	3-2		2-1	0-3	0-1	2-1	1-0	2-0	1-1	1-2	4-3	1-3	2-4	3-2	2-1	2-1	0-1	3-2
Harrow Borough	0-2	1-2	3-2	3-4	0-1	5-0	0-3	2-1		0-4	2-0	1-2	0-5	6-0	0-4	2-2	3-0	3-2	1-2	2-0	2-0	1-1	3-0	1-0
Hendon	4-1	4-2	2-2	0-0	3-3	3-0	3-3	1-0	6-0		1-3	1-4	2-1	1-1	1-1	3-0	2-0	1-0	3-0	4-1	2-1	4-0	0-1	4-3
Kingstonian	0-2	0-1	0-0	0-0	0-1	4-1	1-1	6-0	0-1	0-0		0-4	1-3	3-2	1-3	2-1	1-2	4-0	3-1	0-1	2-1	0-1	2-1	0-0
Leatherhead	1-1	2-1	2-1	1-0	0-1	2-0	1-2	2-1	0-2	1-2	2-0		2-2	2-1	0-2	2-1	1-0	0-1	2-0	0-2	1-0	2-0	4-0	3-0
Leiston	3-1	3-2	2-0	1-0	2-2	2-0	1-5	0-0	3-0	1-2	2-0	1-2		0-1	2-2	3-1	3-0	2-0	2-2	3-1	2-0	2-0	4-0	2-3
Lowestoft Town	1-2	1-2	1-2	0-0	1-3	3-0	0-2	0-3	1-1	2-1	3-1	0-2			0-2	1-0	1-3	2-4	2-4	1-0	1-2	0-0	1-1	1-0
Margate	1-2	4-2	2-0	1-0	1-0	1-1	1-3	4-2	1-1	3-2	0-2	0-0	2-2	1-0		0-2	1-1	3-1	2-0	2-0	0-0	3-2	3-4	1-1
Merstham	0-3	3-3	4-2	1-2	0-4	1-1	2-0	2-0	0-1	1-1	1-2	1-1	1-0	6-2	1-2		0-0	2-1	1-5	2-1	0-1	2-2	4-1	0-4
Metropolitan Police	2-2	1-1	2-0	4-1	1-4	1-1	3-1	2-1	1-0	1-2	3-2	1-2	1-1	0-1	2-2	0-3		3-2	4-2	3-1	2-0	2-0	2-0	3-1
Needham Market	1-1	0-3	3-1	2-0	0-3	2-2	2-2	5-1	0-3	3-3	1-2	0-0	2-5	0-2	3-2	1-3	1-1		1-2	2-1	4-2	1-0	0-1	0-2
Staines Town	0-2	2-1	3-1	0-2	1-1	3-2	4-4	4-1	2-1	4-0	5-0	3-0	1-4	3-1	2-2	4-2	1-5	1-1		5-2	3-1	6-0	0-5	3-3
Thurrock	0-5	3-3	4-2	3-2	0-1	3-1	1-2	1-0	2-0	0-1	1-0	2-0	3-0	0-1	1-1	0-0	1-0	0-2			2-2	4-1	2-4	3-2
Tonbridge Angels	2-1	2-0	0-1	2-0	1-1	1-4	2-3	0-0	2-1	1-0	3-1	0-2	2-1	2-2	0-0	0-1	2-0	5-4	2-1	2-1		1-2	1-0	1-2
Tooting & Mitcham United	2-6	1-1	1-2	1-2	1-3	0-4	0-1	0-1	5-2	0-2	3-2	1-4	0-2	2-5	1-3	3-1	0-2	1-1	0-7	4-1	0-0		2-0	4-3
Wingate & Finchley	1-3	2-1	2-0	2-0	0-0	2-1	2-1	2-0	1-3	2-2	0-1	3-1	0-1	4-3	1-0	3-2	1-0	1-1	0-0	2-4	2-1	1-1		1-0
Worthing	2-1	2-2	2-0	3-1	0-2	2-2	3-2	2-2	2-2	1-2	1-2	1-1	1-1	0-0	0-5	3-2	3-3	1-0	2-2	1-2	2-0	3-0	2-1	

Isthmian League Premier Division

Season 2017/2018

Team	P	W	D	L	F	A	Pts
Billericay Town	46	30	9	7	110	50	99
Dulwich Hamlet	46	28	11	7	91	41	95
Hendon	46	25	10	11	96	59	85
Folkestone Invicta	46	25	10	11	104	71	85
Leiston	46	23	10	13	82	53	79
Leatherhead	46	24	7	15	68	49	79
Margate	46	20	17	9	77	53	77
Staines Town	46	21	12	13	106	83	75
Wingate & Finchley	46	20	9	17	63	71	69
Metropolitan Police	46	19	12	15	76	71	66
Tonbridge Angels	46	19	7	20	58	63	64
Harrow Borough	46	19	6	21	69	76	63
Kingstonian	46	18	5	23	57	70	59
Dorking Wanderers	46	16	10	20	77	80	58
Thurrock	46	17	6	23	68	79	57
Worthing	46	15	12	19	71	84	57
Enfield Town	46	14	14	18	72	80	56
Merstham	46	15	11	20	69	80	56
Needham Market	46	13	10	23	65	84	49
Brightlingsea Regent	46	13	9	24	67	89	48
Harlow Town	46	13	8	25	55	88	47
Lowestoft Town	46	12	7	27	52	92	43
Burgess Hill Town	46	9	9	28	64	102	36
Tooting & Mitcham United	46	9	9	28	52	101	36

Metropolitan Police had 3 points deducted for fielding an ineligible player.

Thurrock resigned from the league at the end of the season.

Promotion Play-offs

Dulwich Hamlet 1   Leiston 0
Hendon 4   Folkestone Invicta 0

Dulwich Hamlet 1   Hendon .... 1 (aet)
Dulwich Hamlet won 4-3 on penalties

Promoted: Billericay Town and Dulwich Hamlet

Relegated: Tooting & Mitcham United

F.A. Trophy 2017/2018

Qualifying 1	Altrincham	3	Clitheroe	0
Qualifying 1	Ashton United	4	Frickley Athletic	1
Qualifying 1	Aylesbury	0	Harlow Town	0
Qualifying 1	Barking	0	Beaconsfield Town	2
Qualifying 1	Barwell	1	Carlton Town	0
Qualifying 1	Biggleswade Town	0	Wingate & Finchley	5
Qualifying 1	Billericay Town	3	Tooting & Mitcham United	1
Qualifying 1	Bishopýs Stortford	4	Hanwell Town	0
Qualifying 1	Bowers & Pitsea	1	Egham Town	1
Qualifying 1	Brentwood Town	0	Bedford Town	0
Qualifying 1	Burgess Hill Town	2	Aveley	0
Qualifying 1	Bury Town	1	Chalfont St Peter	1
Qualifying 1	Buxton	1	Cleethorpes Town	2
Qualifying 1	Cambridge City	0	Alvechurch	2
Qualifying 1	Chasetown	2	Spalding United	1
Qualifying 1	Corinthian-Casuals	3	Hertford Town	1
Qualifying 1	Cray Wanderers	2	Grays Athletic	2
Qualifying 1	Dorchester Town	2	Basingstoke Town	1
Qualifying 1	Dorking Wanderers	5	Ware	0
Qualifying 1	Dunstable Town	1	Lewes	4
Qualifying 1	Farsley Celtic	1	South Shields	1
Qualifying 1	Glossop North End	3	Matlock Town	2
Qualifying 1	Gosport Borough	1	Bristol Manor Farm	0
Qualifying 1	Grantham Town	1	Halesowen Town	0
Qualifying 1	Harrow Borough	1	Haringey Borough	1
Qualifying 1	Hastings United	3	Ashford Town (Middx)	4
Qualifying 1	Hayes & Yeading United	0	Chesham United	3
Qualifying 1	Hednesford Town	1	Mickleover Sports	0
Qualifying 1	Hendon	3	Kings Langley	1
Qualifying 1	Hereford	4	Weymouth	1
Qualifying 1	Hitchin Town	5	Cheshunt	0
Qualifying 1	Kendal Town	2	Atherton Collieries	4
Qualifying 1	Kidlington	1	Slough Town	4
Qualifying 1	Kingstonian	3	Thurrock	3
Qualifying 1	Kingýs Lynn Town	0	Mildenhall Town	1
Qualifying 1	Larkhall Athletic	1	Farnborough	3
Qualifying 1	Leatherhead	1	Hythe Town	0
Qualifying 1	Leek Town	3	Kettering Town	2
Qualifying 1	Leiston	1	Folkestone Invicta	1
Qualifying 1	Maldon & Tiptree	3	Walton Casuals	0
Qualifying 1	Metropolitan Police	3	AFC Sudbury	0
Qualifying 1	Mossley	0	Lancaster City	1
Qualifying 1	Needham Market	3	Arlesey Town	1
Qualifying 1	Newcastle Town	2	Kidsgrove Athletic	2
Qualifying 1	Ossett Town	1	Droylsden	3
Qualifying 1	Paulton Rovers	2	Cirencester Town	2
Qualifying 1	Potters Bar Town	3	Witham Town	0
Qualifying 1	Prescot Cables	0	Stalybridge Celtic	0
Qualifying 1	Redditch United	0	Coalville Town	1
Qualifying 1	Royston Town	2	Enfield Town	0
Qualifying 1	Rushall Olympic	2	Nantwich Town	0
Qualifying 1	Shaw Lane	2	Ramsbottom United	2
Qualifying 1	Shortwood United	2	Frome Town	0
Qualifying 1	Sittingbourne	1	Merstham	1
Qualifying 1	St Neots Town	3	Corby Town	2
Qualifying 1	Stafford Rangers	6	St Ives Town	0

Qualifying 1	Staines Town	0	Margate	3	
Qualifying 1	Stamford	3	Sutton Coldfield Town	0	
Qualifying 1	Stourbridge	1	Basford United	0	
Qualifying 1	Stratford Town	2	Bedworth United	1	
Qualifying 1	Swindon Supermarine	0	Hartley Wintney	3	
Qualifying 1	Taunton Town	2	Merthyr Town	1	
Qualifying 1	Thame United	5	Wimborne Town	0	
Qualifying 1	Thamesmead Town	3	Brightlingsea Regent	1	
Qualifying 1	Tiverton Town	2	Banbury United	2	
Qualifying 1	Tonbridge Angels	3	Heybridge Swifts	3	
Qualifying 1	Waltham Abbey	0	Dulwich Hamlet	3	
Qualifying 1	Warrington Town	2	Bamber Bridge	1	
Qualifying 1	Whitby Town	1	Marine	3	
Qualifying 1	Workington	4	Witton Albion	0	
Qualifying 1	Worthing	3	Lowestoft Town	0	
Qualifying 1	Yate Town	0	Moneyfields	1	
Replay	Banbury United	3	Tiverton Town	2	
Replay	Bedford Town	2	Brentwood Town	4	
Replay	Chalfont St Peter	0	Bury Town	3	
Replay	Cirencester Town	0	Paulton Rovers	4	
Replay	Egham Town	3	Bowers & Pitsea	5	(aet)
	Bowers & Pitsea were subsequently found to have fielded an ineligible player in the first game and were duly disqualified. Egham Town progressed to the second qualifying round.				
Replay	Folkestone Invicta	1	Leiston	1	(aet)
	Leiston won 6-5 on penalties.				
Replay	Grays Athletic	0	Cray Wanderers	2	
Replay	Haringey Borough	1	Harrow Borough	0	
Replay	Harlow Town	4	Aylesbury	2	
Replay	Heybridge Swifts	2	Tonbridge Angels	1	
Replay	Kidsgrove Athletic	2	Newcastle Town	1	
Replay	Merstham	0	Sittingbourne	2	
Replay	Ramsbottom United	4	Shaw Lane	1	(aet)
Replay	South Shields	4	Farsley Celtic	3	(aet)
Replay	Stalybridge Celtic	5	Prescot Cables	1	
Replay	Thurrock	1	Kingstonian	4	
Qualifying 2	Altrincham	4	Ramsbottom United	1	
Qualifying 2	Alvechurch	1	Coalville Town	5	
Qualifying 2	Ashford Town (Middx)	2	Kingstonian	2	
Qualifying 2	Atherton Collieries	1	Marine	5	
Qualifying 2	Barwell	0	Mildenhall Town	1	
Qualifying 2	Billericay Town	6	Bury Town	2	
Qualifying 2	Brentwood Town	3	Needham Market	1	
Qualifying 2	Chasetown	1	Workington	3	
Qualifying 2	Chesham United	3	Hitchin Town	1	
Qualifying 2	Corinthian-Casuals	1	Wingate & Finchley	3	
Qualifying 2	Dorchester Town	1	Heybridge Swifts	2	
Qualifying 2	Dorking Wanderers	4	Leiston	1	
Qualifying 2	Farnborough	3	Banbury United	3	
Qualifying 2	Glossop North End	4	Leek Town	3	
Qualifying 2	Harlow Town	2	Dulwich Hamlet	1	
Qualifying 2	Hartley Wintney	3	Gosport Borough	0	
Qualifying 2	Hednesford Town	1	Cleethorpes Town	1	
Qualifying 2	Hendon	3	Burgess Hill Town	0	
Qualifying 2	Hereford	0	Potters Bar Town	0	
Qualifying 2	Kidsgrove Athletic	0	Grantham Town	2	
Qualifying 2	Lancaster City	3	Stratford Town	0	
Qualifying 2	Lewes	2	Bishop's Stortford	0	
Qualifying 2	Maldon & Tiptree	1	Slough Town	4	

Qualifying 2	Margate	2	Egham Town	0	
Qualifying 2	Moneyfields	1	Cray Wanderers	1	
Qualifying 2	Paulton Rovers	1	Shortwood United	2	
Qualifying 2	Royston Town	3	Leatherhead	2	
Qualifying 2	Sittingbourne	1	Haringey Borough	1	
Qualifying 2	St Neots Town	2	Stourbridge	3	
Qualifying 2	Stafford Rangers	3	South Shields	1	
Qualifying 2	Stalybridge Celtic	3	Rushall Olympic	2	
Qualifying 2	Stamford	1	Droylsden	2	
Qualifying 2	Taunton Town	1	Beaconsfield Town	1	
Qualifying 2	Thame United	1	Worthing	0	
Qualifying 2	Thamesmead Town	0	Metropolitan Police	1	
Qualifying 2	Warrington Town	1	Ashton United	1	
Replay	Ashton United	2	Warrington Town	2	(aet)
	Warrington Town won 4-2 on penalties.				
Replay	Banbury United	2	Farnborough	3	(aet)
Replay	Beaconsfield Town	1	Taunton Town	1	(aet)
	Taunton Town won 7-6 on penalties.				
Replay	Cleethorpes Town	2	Hednesford Town	1	
Replay	Cray Wanderers	4	Moneyfields	1	
Replay	Haringey Borough	1	Sittingbourne	0	
Replay	Kingstonian	2	Ashford Town (Middx)	0	
Replay	Potters Bar Town	1	Hereford	2	
Qualifying 3	AFC Telford United	4	Droylsden	2	
Qualifying 3	Alfreton Town	0	Altrincham	2	
Qualifying 3	Bath City	0	Margate	0	
Qualifying 3	Blyth Spartans	2	Stalybridge Celtic	1	
Qualifying 3	Boston United	2	Kidderminster Harriers	2	
Qualifying 3	Brackley Town	4	Salford City	0	
Qualifying 3	Bradford (Park Avenue)	1	Stourbridge	1	
Qualifying 3	Braintree Town	3	Cray Wanderers	0	
Qualifying 3	Brentwood Town	1	Dartford	2	
Qualifying 3	Chesham United	2	Gloucester City	1	
Qualifying 3	Cleethorpes Town	1	Spennymoor Town	2	
Qualifying 3	Darlington	2	Harrogate Town	3	
Qualifying 3	East Thurrock United	3	Shortwood United	1	
Qualifying 3	Eastbourne Borough	1	Royston Town	1	
Qualifying 3	Farnborough	1	Hartley Wintney	2	
Qualifying 3	Gainsborough Trinity	2	Stafford Rangers	0	
Qualifying 3	Glossop North End	0	Workington	0	
Qualifying 3	Grantham Town	3	Chorley	4	
Qualifying 3	Hampton & Richmond Borough	5	Harlow Town	1	
Qualifying 3	Haringey Borough	3	Thame United	1	
Qualifying 3	Havant & Waterlooville	3	Dorking Wanderers	1	
Qualifying 3	Hemel Hempstead Town	1	Bognor Regis Town	1	
Qualifying 3	Hendon	1	Slough Town	1	
Qualifying 3	Heybridge Swifts	5	Kingstonian	1	
Qualifying 3	Hungerford Town	0	Billericay Town	2	
Qualifying 3	Kingstonian	2	Heybridge Swifts	2	
Qualifying 3	Lancaster City	1	Mildenhall Town	0	
Qualifying 3	Leamington	3	Curzon Ashton	1	
Qualifying 3	Lewes	1	Truro City	3	
Qualifying 3	Marine	1	FC United Of Manchester	0	
Qualifying 3	Metropolitan Police	0	Wingate & Finchley	1	
Qualifying 3	Nuneaton Town	5	North Ferriby United	1	
Qualifying 3	Oxford City	1	Hereford	2	
Qualifying 3	St Albans City	3	Poole Town	1	

Qualifying 3	Stockport County	2	Southport	2	
Qualifying 3	Tamworth	2	Warrington Town	2	
Qualifying 3	Taunton Town	3	Concord Rangers	2	
Qualifying 3	Wealdstone	1	Chelmsford City	1	
Qualifying 3	Welling United	0	Weston Super Mare	1	
Qualifying 3	Whitehawk	2	Chippenham Town	1	
Qualifying 3	York City	3	Coalville Town	1	
Replay	Bognor Regis Town	1	Hemel Hempstead Town	0	
Replay	Chelmsford City	1	Wealdstone	2	
Replay	Kidderminster Harriers	2	Boston United	0	
Replay	Margate	2	Bath City	2	(aet)
	Bath City won 5-4 on penalties.				
Replay	Royston Town	2	Eastbourne Borough	2	(aet)
	Eastbourne Borough won 4-3 on penalties.				
Replay	Slough Town	1	Hendon	1	(aet)
	Hendon won 3-0 on penalties.				
Replay	Southport	0	Stockport County	3	
Replay	Stourbridge	2	Bradford (Park Avenue)	1	
Replay	Warrington Town	3	Tamworth	0	
Replay	Workington	5	Glossop North End	1	
Round 1	Billericay Town	3	Havant & Waterlooville	1	
Round 1	Blyth Spartans	1	AFC Telford United	0	
Round 1	Braintree Town	0	Brackley Town	0	
Round 1	Chesham United	0	Weston Super Mare	2	
Round 1	Chester	2	AFC Fylde	2	(aet)
	Chester won 5-4 on penalties.				
Round 1	Chorley	1	Marine	3	
Round 1	Dartford	1	Boreham Wood	1	
Round 1	Dover Athletic	3	Eastbourne Borough	0	
Round 1	East Thurrock United	4	Aldershot Town	0	
Round 1	Ebbsfleet United	2	Eastleigh	1	
Round 1	FC Halifax Town	1	Macclesfield Town	0	
Round 1	Gateshead	2	Guiseley	1	(aet)
Round 1	Hampton & Richmond Borough	1	Heybridge Swifts	1	
Round 1	Haringey Borough	1	Leyton Orient	2	
Round 1	Hartley Wintney	0	Bromley	2	
Round 1	Hendon	2	Bath City	1	
Round 1	Hereford	3	Dagenham & Redbridge	2	
Round 1	Kidderminster Harriers	2	York City	1	
Round 1	Lancaster City	1	Stockport County	3	
Round 1	Leamington	0	Stourbridge	1	
Round 1	Nuneaton Town	0	Barrow	1	
Round 1	Solihull Moors	2	Tranmere Rovers	0	
Round 1	Spennymoor Town	4	Gainsborough Trinity	4	(aet)
	Spennymoor Town won 5-3 on penalties.				
Round 1	Sutton United	1	Truro City	0	
Round 1	Taunton Town	1	Bognor Regis Town	4	
Round 1	Torquay United	0	Maidstone United	4	
Round 1	Warrington Town	0	Altrincham	0	
Round 1	Wealdstone	1	Wingate & Finchley	0	
Round 1	Whitehawk	1	St Albans City	2	
Round 1	Woking	0	Maidenhead United	2	
Round 1	Workington	1	Hartlepool United	0	
Round 1	Wrexham	0	Harrogate Town	2	
Replay	Altrincham	1	Warrington Town	2	
Replay	Boreham Wood	2	Dartford	2	(aet)
	Boreham Wood won 3-1 on penalties.				

Replay	Brackley Town	2	Braintree Town	0	
Replay	Heybridge Swifts	3	Hampton & Richmond Borough	2	
Round 2	Billericay Town	3	Stourbridge	2	
Round 2	Blyth Spartans	1	Bromley	4	
Round 2	Bognor Regis Town	1	Leyton Orient	2	(aet)
Round 2	Brackley Town	0	Barrow	0	
Round 2	Dover Athletic	4	Marine	3	
Round 2	East Thurrock United	1	Chester	0	
Round 2	Ebbsfleet United	1	Warrington Town	1	
Round 2	FC Halifax Town	1	Maidenhead United	4	
Round 2	Gateshead	3	Boreham Wood	3	
Round 2	Kidderminster Harriers	2	Stockport County	2	
Round 2	Maidstone United	2	Heybridge Swifts	1	
Round 2	Spennymoor Town	2	Solihull Moors	0	
Round 2	St Albans City	1	Harrogate Town	1	
Round 2	Sutton United	3	Hendon	0	
Round 2	Wealdstone	1	Hereford	0	
Round 2	Weston Super Mare	1	Workington	1	
Replay	Barrow	0	Brackley Town	2	
Replay	Boreham Wood	1	Gateshead	2	
Replay	Harrogate Town	5	St Albans City	0	
Replay	Stockport County	3	Kidderminster Harriers	0	
Replay	Warrington Town	2	Ebbsfleet United	0	
Replay	Workington	2	Weston Super Mare	1	
Round 3	Brackley Town	3	Sutton United	1	
Round 3	Dover Athletic	3	Leyton Orient	4	
Round 3	Harrogate Town	2	Billericay Town	2	
Round 3	Maidenhead United	1	Stockport County	1	
Round 3	Maidstone United	2	Gateshead	2	
Round 3	Spennymoor Town	1	East Thurrock United	1	
Round 3	Wealdstone	2	Warrington Town	1	
Round 3	Workington	1	Bromley	1	
Replay	Billericay Town	3	Harrogate Town	2	
Replay	Bromley	7	Workington	1	
Replay	East Thurrock United	2	Spennymoor Town	5	
Replay	Gateshead	3	Maidstone United	0	
Replay	Stockport County	3	Maidenhead United	2	(aet)
Round 4	Billericay Town	2	Wealdstone	5	
Round 4	Bromley	0	Spennymoor Town	0	
Round 4	Leyton Orient	3	Gateshead	3	
Round 4	Stockport County	1	Brackley Town	1	
Replay	Brackley Town	2	Stockport County	1	
Replay	Gateshead	3	Leyton Orient	2	
Replay	Spennymoor Town	1	Bromley	2	
	Played at Blackwell Meadows, Darlington				

Semi-finals

1st leg	Brackley Town	1	Wealdstone	0	
1st leg	Bromley	3	Gateshead	2	
2nd leg	Gateshead	1	Bromley	1	
	Bromley won 4-3 on aggregate.				
2nd leg	Wealdstone	0	Brackley Town	2	
	Brackley Town won 3-0 on aggregate.				
FINAL	Brackley Town	1	Bromley	1	(aet)
	Brackley Town won 5-4 on penalties.				

F.A. Vase 2017/2018

Round	Home	Score	Away	Score	Notes
Round 1	AFC Darwen	2	Marske United	3	
Round 1	AFC Emley	2	Thornaby	6	
Round 1	AFC Portchester	2	Cullompton Rangers	3	
Round 1	AFC Wulfrunians	1	Leicester Nirvana	1	(aet)
Round 1	Alsager Town	5	Runcorn Town	2	
Round 1	Ashington	1	Hall Road Rangers	2	
Round 1	Ashton Athletic	4	Liversedge	2	
Round 1	Baffins Milton Rovers	1	Radstock Town	0	
Round 1	Balham	1	Deal Town	3	
Round 1	Bardon Hill	3	Quorn	4	
Round 1	Bashley	2	Bridgwater Town	3	(aet)
Round 1	Basildon United	0	Biggleswade	2	
Round 1	Beckenham Town	2	Sawbridgeworth Town	0	
Round 1	Bedlington Terriers	1	Charnock Richard	0	
Round 1	Biggleswade United	0	Yaxley	1	
Round 1	Blaby & Whetstone Athletic	3	Northampton On Chenecks	1	
Round 1	Bodmin Town	2	Swanage Town & Herston	1	
Round 1	Bracknell Town	6	Buckingham Athletic	2	
Round 1	Broadbridge Heath	3	Kensington Borough	0	
Round 1	Brockenhurst	2	Crediton United	1	(aet)
Round 1	Brocton	4	Wednesfield	1	
Round 1	Burnham Ramblers	0	Leighton Town	1	
Round 1	Canterbury City	4	K Sports	3	
Round 1	Christchurch	3	United Services Portsmouth	0	
Round 1	City of Liverpool	7	Dronfield Town	0	
Round 1	Cobham	0	Westfield	4	
Round 1	Crawley Green	3	Harpenden Town	0	
Round 1	Cray Valley Paper Mill	3	Cricklewood Wanderers	1	

Cray Valley were subsequently disqualified for fielding an ineligible player. Cricklewood Wanderers progressed to Round 2.

Round	Home	Score	Away	Score	Notes
Round 1	Dunston UTS	2	Burscough	1	
Round 1	Eastwood Community	3	Dunkirk	2	
Round 1	Edgware Town	1	Walton & Hersham	3	
Round 1	Enfield 1893	1	Coggeshall Town	0	(aet)
Round 1	Enfield Borough	4	Newmarket Town	2	
Round 1	Erith & Belvedere	2	Horley Town	2	(aet)
Round 1	Erith Town	4	Pagham	0	
Round 1	FC Bolsover	1	Deeping Rangers	3	
Round 1	FC Romania	2	Eynesbury Rovers	0	
Round 1	Fareham Town	4	Ivybridge Town	3	
Round 1	Farnham Town	2	Lymington Town	0	
Round 1	Flackwell Heath	2	Windsor	5	
Round 1	Framlingham Town	2	Cockfosters	0	
Round 1	Frimley Green	0	Blackfield & Langley	2	
Round 1	Garforth Town	2	Knaresborough Town	3	(aet)
Round 1	Halstead Town	2	Tower Hamlets	2	(aet)

Tower Hamlets won 6-5 on penalties.

Round	Home	Score	Away	Score	Notes
Round 1	Hanley Town	1	Godmanchester Rovers	3	
Round 1	Hanworth Villa	3	Three Bridges	2	
Round 1	Haughmond	1	Worksop Town	2	
Round 1	Haywards Heath Town	2	Camberley Town	0	
Round 1	Hengrove Athletic	4	Alton Town	2	(aet)
Round 1	Highworth Town	1	Sholing	3	
Round 1	Holbeach United	1	South Normanton Athletic	0	
Round 1	Holland	1	Great Wakering Rovers	2	
Round 1	Hullbridge Sports	1	Colney Heath	1	(aet)

Round 1	Irlam	1	1874 Northwich	4	
Round 1	London Colney	4	Cogenhoe United	4	(aet)
Round 1	London Lions	3	Clapton	2	
Round 1	Lutterworth Town	2	Coventry United	3	
Round 1	Meridian VP	2	Hollands & Blair	0	
Round 1	Newport (IOW)	7	Bovey Tracey	2	
Round 1	North Shields	4	Handsworth Parramore	2	
Round 1	Norwich CBS	1	Oxhey Jets	0	
Round 1	Odd Down	1	Tavistock	2	
Round 1	Peterborough Northern Star	1	Baldock Town	0	
Round 1	Pickering Town	3	Newcastle Benfield	4	(aet)
Round 1	Pinxton	3	Heather St Johns	1	
Round 1	Plymouth Parkway	6	Sandhurst Town	1	
Round 1	Pontefract Collieries	3	Litherland Remyca	1	
Round 1	Portland United	0	Horndean	1	
Round 1	Racing Club Warwick	2	Clipstone	0	
Round 1	Romsey Town	2	Hamble Club	3	
Round 1	Rossington Main	3	Bootle	4	(aet)
Round 1	Royal Wootton Bassett Town	2	Ampthill Town	1	
Round 1	Rugby Town	2	Harrowby United	0	(aet)
Round 1	Rushden & Higham United	0	Highgate United	2	
Round 1	Rusthall	2	Epsom & Ewell	7	
Round 1	Saltdean United	0	Whitstable Town	1	(aet)
Round 1	Sevenoaks Town	2	Longlevens	1	
Round 1	Sheppey United	2	Fisher	1	
Round 1	Spelthorne Sports	0	Lordswood	1	
Round 1	Stafford Town	0	Kimberley MW	1	
Round 1	Stourport Swifts	3	Shirebrook Town	2	
Round 1	Sunderland Ryhope CW	10	Harrogate Railway Athletic	1	
Round 1	Team Northumbria	1	Runcorn Linnets	1	(aet)
Round 1	Thatcham Town	2	Horsham YMCA	1	
Round 1	Thetford Town	1	Debenham LC	1	(aet)
Round 1	Tow Law Town	2	Bridlington Town	1	
Round 1	Walsall Wood	1	Atherstone Town	0	
Round 1	Wantage Town	4	Cadbury Heath	3	
Round 1	Wellington	0	Desborough Town	2	
Round 1	Wellington AFC	4	Downton	3	(aet)
Round 1	Welwyn Garden City	3	Takeley	0	
Round 1	Wembley	3	Broadfields United	0	
Round 1	West Didsbury & Chorlton	0	West Auckland Town	3	
Round 1	Westella & Willerby	1	Whitley Bay	5	
Round 1	Westfields	6	Shifnal Town	0	
Round 1	Whickham	0	Stockton Town	2	
Round 1	Willand Rovers	7	Street	1	
Round 1	Wisbech St Mary	2	Whitton United	1	
Round 1	Wisbech Town	4	Felixstowe & Walton United	0	
Round 1	Wolverhampton SC	4	Staveley MW	2	
Round 1	Worcester City	4	Sherwood Colliery	3	
Replay	Cogenhoe United	1	London Colney	0	
Replay	Colney Heath	0	Hullbridge Sports	1	
Replay	Debenham LC	0	Thetford Town	2	
Replay	Horley Town	3	Erith & Belvedere	2	(aet)
Replay	Leicester Nirvana	4	AFC Wulfrunians	1	
Replay	Runcorn Linnets	3	Team Northumbria	2	

Round 2	1874 Northwich	5	Tow Law Town	1	
Round 2	Ashton Athletic	1	Morpeth Town	0	
Round 2	Baffins Milton Rovers	3	Cullompton Rangers	1	
Round 2	Bedlington Terriers	0	Newcastle Benfield	3	
Round 2	Biggleswade	2	Crawley Green	0	
Round 2	Bracknell Town	8	Cricklewood Wanderers	0	
Round 2	Brocton	3	Shepshed Dynamo	5	
Round 2	Buckland Athletic	1	Bradford Town	2	
Round 2	Chichester City	3	Deal Town	0	
Round 2	Christchurch	3	Fareham Town	2	
Round 2	Sun Sports		Cogenhoe United		

Sun Sports were exempted to the second-round proper but resigned from first-team football after the season started. Cogenhoe United received a bye to Round 3.

Round 2	Coleshill Town	8	Blaby & Whetstone Athletic	1	
Round 2	Corinthian	3	Eastbourne Town	4	
Round 2	Crowborough Athletic	5	Croydon	0	
Round 2	Desborough Town	7	Pinxton	4	(aet)
Round 2	Dunston UTS	0	Worksop Town	1	
Round 2	Enfield Borough	2	Berkhamsted	4	(aet)
Round 2	Erith Town	1	Windsor	2	
Round 2	Exmouth Town	1	Blackfield & Langley	3	
Round 2	Farnham Town	2	Bridgwater Town	3	
Round 2	Godmanchester Rovers	3	Deeping Rangers	4	
Round 2	Gorleston	2	Framlingham Town	1	
Round 2	Great Wakering Rovers	2	FC Romania	2	(aet)
Round 2	Hall Road Rangers	2	Pontefract Collieries	4	
Round 2	Hamble Club	5	Brockenhurst	4	(aet)
Round 2	Haywards Heath Town	1	Sevenoaks Town	2	
Round 2	Hinckley	2	AFC Mansfield	0	
Round 2	Horndean	3	Royal Wootton Bassett Town	2	
Round 2	Hullbridge Sports	3	Wembley	2	
Round 2	Kimberley MW	0	Stourport Swifts	2	
Round 2	Leicester Nirvana	0	Eastwood Community	2	
Round 2	Leighton Town	1	London Lions	0	
Round 2	Marske United	2	Shildon	1	(aet)
Round 2	Meridian VP	0	Horley Town	3	
Round 2	Newport (IOW)	6	Hengrove Athletic	2	
Round 2	North Shields	2	Knaresborough Town	1	
Round 2	Plymouth Parkway	4	Bodmin Town	2	
Round 2	Quorn	0	Coventry United	6	
Round 2	Racing Club Warwick	2	Alsager Town	1	
Round 2	Runcorn Linnets	1	Sunderland RCA	1	(aet)
Round 2	Sheppey United	2	Beckenham Town	3	
Round 2	Sholing	2	Wellington AFC	1	
Round 2	Southall	1	Lordswood	2	
Round 2	Sporting Khalsa	0	Bromsgrove Sporting	1	
Round 2	Stockton Town	4	Bootle	2	(aet)
Round 2	Sunderland Ryhope CW	1	City of Liverpool	2	
Round 2	Team Solent	2	Tavistock	0	
Round 2	Thatcham Town	8	Broadbridge Heath	2	
Round 2	Thetford Town	1	Wisbech Town	4	
Round 2	Thornaby	2	Whitley Bay	4	
Round 2	Tower Hamlets	1	Enfield 1893	2	
Round 2	Tring Athletic	4	Ely City	1	
Round 2	Walsall Wood	5	Holbeach United	0	
Round 2	Walton & Hersham	2	Hanworth Villa	1	

Round 2	Wantage Town	1	Melksham Town	4	
Round 2	Welwyn Garden City	2	Newport Pagnell Town	1	
Round 2	West Auckland Town	3	Billingham Town	2	
Round 2	Westfield	1	Canterbury City	0	
Round 2	Whitstable Town	3	Epsom & Ewell	2	(aet)
Round 2	Willand Rovers	1	Westfields	3	
Round 2	Wisbech St Mary	1	Norwich CBS	4	
Round 2	Wolverhampton SC	2	Rugby Town	2	(aet)
Round 2	Worcester City	1	Highgate United	2	
Round 2	Yaxley	3	Peterborough Northern Star	0	
Replay	FC Romania	0	Great Wakering Rovers	1	
Replay	Rugby Town	0	Wolverhampton SC	2	
Replay	Sunderland RCA	1	Runcorn Linnets	2	
Round 3	1874 Northwich	2	Ashton Athletic	0	
Round 3	Beckenham Town	2	Eastbourne Town	3	
Round 3	Bradford Town	4	Team Solent	0	
Round 3	Bridgwater Town	2	Melksham Town	2	(aet)
Round 3	Bromsgrove Sporting	1	Coventry United	1	(aet)
Round 3	Christchurch	0	Newport (IOW)	1	
Round 3	Crowborough Athletic	1	Westfield	0	
Round 3	Desborough Town	4	Eastwood Community	1	
Round 3	Gorleston	2	Leighton Town	4	
Round 3	Great Wakering Rovers	0	Cogenhoe United	2	
Round 3	Hamble Club	2	Horndean	1	
Round 3	Highgate United	1	Coleshill Town	0	
Round 3	Hinckley	3	Deeping Rangers	1	
Round 3	Horley Town	4	Baffins Milton Rovers	1	
Round 3	Hullbridge Sports	3	Enfield 1893	2	
Round 3	Lordswood	0	Bracknell Town	1	
Round 3	Newcastle Benfield	3	North Shields	1	
Round 3	Plymouth Parkway	2	Westfields	3	
Round 3	Pontefract Collieries	3	Worksop Town	0	
Round 3	Racing Club Warwick	0	Wisbech Town	2	
Round 3	Runcorn Linnets	2	Marske United	3	
Round 3	Sholing	0	Blackfield & Langley	1	
Round 3	Stockton Town	1	City Of Liverpool	0	
Round 3	Stourport Swifts	3	Walsall Wood	1	
Round 3	Thatcham Town	3	Sevenoaks Town	1	
Round 3	Tring Athletic	1	Berkhamsted	0	
Round 3	Walton & Hersham	1	Windsor	2	
Round 3	Welwyn Garden City	1	Biggleswade	2	
Round 3	West Auckland Town	4	Whitley Bay	3	
Round 3	Whitstable Town	0	Chichester City	2	
Round 3	Wolverhampton SC	5	Shepshed Dynamo	0	
Round 3	Yaxley	2	Norwich CBS	3	
Replay	Coventry United	3	Bromsgrove Sporting	3	(aet)
	Bromsgrove Sporting won 4-3 on penalties.				
Replay	Melksham Town	2	Bridgwater Town	0	
Round 4	1874 Northwich	3	Pontefract Collieries	1	
Round 4	Blackfield & Langley	3	Bracknell Town	3	(aet)
Round 4	Cogenhoe United	2	Wolverhampton SC	3	

90

Round 4	Coleshill Town	1	Newcastle Benfield	1	(aet)
	Coleshill Town won 4-2 on penalties.				
Round 4	Desborough Town	2	Stourport Swifts	4	(aet)
Round 4	Eastbourne Town	1	Windsor	3	
Round 4	Horley Town	1	Chichester City	2	
Round 4	Leighton Town	5	Norwich CBS	2	(aet)
Round 4	Marske United	5	Hinckley	0	
Round 4	Melksham Town	2	Crowborough Athletic	1	
Round 4	Newcastle Benfield	1	Coleshill Town	1	(aet)
Round 4	Newport (IOW)	0	Bradford Town	1	
Round 4	Stockton Town	2	West Auckland Town	1	(aet)
Round 4	Thatcham Town	2	Biggleswade	1	
Round 4	Tring Athletic	5	Hullbridge Sports	1	
Round 4	Westfields	1	Hamble Club	4	
Round 4	Wisbech Town	1	Bromsgrove Sporting	3	
Replay	Bracknell Town	2	Blackfield & Langley	1	
Round 5	1874 Northwich	1	Chichester City	0	
Round 5	Coleshill Town	2	Bracknell Town	4	(aet)
Round 5	Marske United	2	Bradford Town	0	
Round 5	Melksham Town	2	Tring Athletic	1	
Round 5	Stockton Town	3	Stourport Swifts	0	
Round 5	Thatcham Town	2	Bromsgrove Sporting	1	
Round 5	Windsor	2	Hamble Club	0	
Round 5	Wolverhampton SC	3	Leighton Town	4	
Round 6	Bracknell Town	0	Marske United	3	
Round 6	Leighton Town	0	1874 Northwich	1	
Round 6	Melksham Town	0	Thatcham Town	1	
Round 6	Stockton Town	2	Windsor	0	
Semi-finals					
1st leg	Stockton Town	2	Marske United	0	
1st leg	Thatcham Town	1	1874 Northwich	0	
2nd leg	1874 Northwich	2	Thatcham Town	3	
	Thatcham Town won 4-2 on aggregate.				
2nd leg	Stockton Town	1	Marske United	2	
	Stockton Town won 3-2 on aggregate.				
FINAL	Thatcham Town	1	Stockton Town	0	

Cup Statistics provided by:

www.soccerdata.com

National League Fixtures 2018/2019	AFC Fylde	Aldershot Town	Barnet	Barrow	Boreham Wood	Braintree Town	Bromley	Chesterfield	Dagenham & Redbridge	Dover Athletic	Eastleigh	Ebbsfleet United	FC Halifax Town	Gateshead	Harrogate Town	Hartlepool United	Havant & Waterlooville	Leyton Orient	Maidenhead United	Maidstone United	Salford City	Solihull Moors	Sutton United	Wrexham
AFC Fylde		15/09	19/04	01/01	24/11	29/09	04/08	16/02	16/03	18/08	06/04	22/12	27/04	30/10	27/08	12/03	02/02	03/11	02/03	13/10	04/09	14/08	01/12	19/01
Aldershot Town	30/03		04/08	24/11	30/10	03/11	08/09	19/01	14/08	22/09	09/02	01/12	06/10	02/03	18/08	13/04	22/04	12/03	01/01	25/09	16/03	02/02	27/08	22/12
Barnet	22/09	05/01		02/03	01/01	07/08	22/04	01/12	27/08	22/12	11/08	18/08	12/03	24/11	26/01	16/03	25/09	30/03	08/09	03/11	30/10	06/10	09/02	13/04
Barrow	26/12	09/03	27/10		30/03	25/08	09/02	14/08	08/09	13/04	17/11	23/02	19/01	25/09	23/03	22/04	04/08	02/02	22/09	08/12	29/12	01/09	06/10	27/11
Boreham Wood	09/03	23/03	26/12	15/09		01/09	27/10	04/09	04/08	27/11	27/04	17/11	25/08	14/08	29/09	16/02	19/01	08/12	13/10	29/12	19/04	23/02	06/04	02/02
Braintree Town	13/04	23/02	19/01	01/12	22/12		23/03	02/02	22/04	27/10	06/10	01/01	04/08	30/03	09/03	14/08	18/08	25/09	27/08	22/09	09/02	17/11	27/11	08/09
Bromley	05/01	06/04	04/09	13/10	02/03	30/10		12/03	24/11	07/08	26/01	27/04	29/09	18/08	11/08	03/11	27/08	16/03	22/12	16/02	15/09	19/04	01/01	01/12
Chesterfield	06/10	07/08	25/08	26/01	22/04	11/08	27/11		30/03	08/09	09/03	05/01	09/02	22/09	23/02	29/12	17/11	01/09	25/09	13/04	08/12	26/12	23/03	27/10
Dagenham & Red.	17/11	26/01	29/12	06/04	05/01	04/09	09/03	15/09		23/03	19/04	29/09	08/12	16/02	27/10	25/08	27/11	26/12	11/08	07/08	01/09	27/04	23/02	13/10
Dover Athletic	08/12	19/04	01/09	29/09	12/03	02/03	19/01	06/04	30/10		25/08	04/09	16/03	02/02	09/02	24/11	14/08	29/12	03/11	26/12	06/10	15/09	27/04	04/08
Eastleigh	08/09	13/10	02/02	16/03	25/09	16/02	14/08	24/11	22/09	01/12		27/08	02/03	13/04	22/12	30/03	01/01	30/10	22/04	12/03	03/11	04/08	19/01	18/08
Ebbsfleet United	01/09	25/08	08/12	03/11	16/03	26/12	25/09	04/08	13/04	22/04	29/12		24/11	08/09	06/10	02/02	22/09	19/01	12/03	30/10	02/03	09/02	14/08	30/03
FC Halifax Town	25/09	16/02	27/11	07/08	01/12	05/01	13/04	13/10	18/08	17/11	27/10	09/03		27/08	01/01	22/09	23/02	08/09	30/03	11/08	26/01	23/03	22/12	22/04
Gateshead	23/03	27/10	09/03	27/04	26/01	15/09	08/12	19/04	06/10	11/08	29/09	06/04	29/12		04/09	26/12	09/02	25/08	05/01	01/09	07/08	27/11	17/11	23/02
Harrogate Town	29/12	08/12	14/08	30/10	13/04	24/11	02/02	03/11	02/03	13/10	01/09	16/02	26/12	22/04		19/01	08/09	22/09	16/03	30/03	12/03	25/08	04/08	25/09
Hartlepool United	27/11	29/09	17/11	04/09	06/10	26/01	23/02	27/08	01/12	09/03	15/09	11/08	19/04	01/01	07/08		22/12	09/02	18/08	05/01	27/04	06/04	27/10	23/03
Havant & Waterloo.	11/08	04/09	27/04	05/01	07/08	08/12	29/12	16/03	12/03	26/01	26/12	19/04	03/11	13/10	06/04	01/09		02/03	30/10	24/11	25/08	29/09	15/09	16/02
Leyton Orient	23/02	27/11	15/09	11/08	18/08	27/04	17/11	22/12	01/01	27/08	23/03	07/08	06/04	01/12	19/04	13/10	27/10		16/02	26/01	05/01	04/09	29/09	09/03
Maidenhead United	27/10	26/12	06/04	19/04	09/02	29/12	01/09	27/04	02/02	23/02	04/09	27/11	15/09	04/08	17/11	08/12	23/03	06/10		25/08	29/09	19/01	09/03	14/08
Maidstone United	09/02	27/04	23/02	18/08	27/08	19/04	06/10	29/09	19/01	01/01	27/11	23/03	02/02	22/12	15/09	04/08	09/03	14/08	01/12		06/04	27/10	04/09	17/11
Salford City	22/04	17/11	23/03	27/08	22/09	13/10	30/03	18/08	22/12	16/02	23/02	27/10	14/08	19/01	27/11	25/09	01/12	04/08	13/04	08/09		09/03	02/02	01/01
Solihull Moors	26/01	11/08	16/02	22/12	03/11	16/03	22/09	01/01	25/09	30/03	05/01	13/10	30/10	12/03	01/12	08/09	13/04	22/04	07/08	02/03	24/11		18/08	27/08
Sutton United	25/08	29/12	13/10	16/02	08/09	12/03	26/12	30/10	03/11	25/09	07/08	26/01	01/09	16/03	05/01	02/03	30/03	13/04	24/11	22/04	11/08	08/12		22/09
Wrexham	07/08	01/09	29/09	12/03	11/08	06/04	25/08	02/03	09/02	05/01	08/12	15/09	04/09	03/11	27/04	30/10	06/10	24/11	26/01	16/03	26/12	29/12	19/04	

Please note that the above fixtures may be subject to change.

National League North Fixtures 2018/2019	AFC Telford United	Alfreton Town	Altrincham	Ashton United	Blyth Spartans	Boston United	Brackley Town	Bradford Park Avenue	Chester	Chorley	Curzon Ashton	Darlington	FC United of Manchester	Guiseley	Hereford	Kidderminster Harriers	Leamington	Nuneaton Borough	Southport	Spennymoor Town	Stockport County	York City
AFC Telford United		22/04	23/03	01/09	30/03	10/11	14/08	01/12	25/08	13/10	13/04	23/02	09/03	02/02	30/10	19/01	29/12	26/12	04/08	05/01	15/09	27/10
Alfreton Town	03/11		06/04	02/03	18/08	01/01	19/01	29/09	27/04	16/02	14/08	12/01	20/04	08/09	16/03	04/08	20/10	17/11	27/08	08/12	22/12	02/02
Altrincham	08/12	13/10		27/10	12/01	18/08	16/03	16/02	02/03	13/04	08/09	22/12	14/08	27/08	22/04	30/03	04/08	30/10	19/01	02/02	01/01	17/11
Ashton United	12/01	10/11	27/04		23/03	03/11	18/08	09/03	20/04	08/09	01/01	27/08	19/01	20/10	16/02	02/02	29/09	04/08	22/12	06/04	01/12	14/08
Blyth Spartans	29/09	05/01	01/09	08/12		06/04	02/03	07/08	11/08	25/08	17/11	09/02	03/11	20/04	26/01	23/02	15/09	16/03	27/04	26/12	20/10	29/12
Boston United	02/03	26/12	05/01	22/04	13/10		30/10	29/12	15/09	16/03	30/03	13/04	02/02	04/08	27/10	01/09	19/01	14/08	17/11	25/08	23/02	08/12
Brackley Town	09/02	07/08	01/12	05/01	10/11	20/04		26/01	03/11	01/09	16/02	11/08	27/04	06/04	08/09	23/03	26/12	29/12	29/09	20/10	09/03	25/08
Bradford Park Ave	16/03	30/03	15/09	17/11	19/01	27/08	04/08		23/02	27/10	02/03	30/10	12/01	01/01	22/12	13/10	02/02	13/04	08/12	14/08	18/08	22/04
Chester	22/12	27/10	10/11	30/10	02/02	16/02	22/04	08/09		30/03	19/01	01/12	18/08	12/01	27/08	14/08	09/03	13/10	01/01	04/08	23/03	13/04
Chorley	06/04	15/09	20/10	23/02	22/12	01/12	12/01	27/04	29/09		27/08	10/11	01/01	19/01	18/08	09/03	23/03	02/02	14/08	03/11	20/04	04/08
Curzon Ashton	20/10	09/02	23/02	26/12	09/03	29/09	15/09	10/11	06/08	29/12		26/01	23/03	01/12	11/08	25/08	06/04	01/09	20/04	27/04	03/11	05/01
Darlington	08/09	01/09	25/08	29/12	15/08	20/10	02/02	20/04	16/03	02/03	04/08		06/04	03/11	17/11	05/01	27/04	08/12	16/02	19/01	29/09	26/12
FC United of Man.	17/11	30/10	09/02	07/08	22/04	11/08	27/10	01/09	05/01	26/12	08/12	13/10		16/02	02/03	13/04	25/08	30/03	08/09	29/12	26/01	16/03
Guiseley	11/08	23/02	29/12	13/04	30/10	26/01	13/10	26/12	01/09	07/08	16/03	22/04	15/09		08/12	27/10	05/01	25/08	02/03	17/11	09/02	30/03
Hereford	20/04	01/12	03/11	15/09	04/08	27/04	23/02	25/08	29/12	05/01	02/02	09/03	10/11	23/03		26/12	14/08	19/01	20/10	29/09	06/04	01/09
Kidderminster Harr.	07/08	26/01	29/09	11/08	08/09	12/01	08/12	06/04	09/02	17/11	22/12	18/08	20/10	27/04	01/01		20/04	02/03	03/11	16/03	27/08	16/02
Leamington	27/08	13/04	26/01	30/03	16/02	07/08	01/01	11/08	17/11	08/12	13/10	27/10	22/12	18/08	09/02	30/10		22/04	16/03	08/09	12/01	02/03
Nuneaton Borough	01/01	09/03	20/04	26/01	01/12	09/02	27/08	20/10	06/04	11/08	12/01	23/03	29/09	22/12	07/08	10/11	03/11		18/08	16/02	27/04	08/09
Southport	26/01	29/12	07/08	25/08	27/10	09/03	30/03	23/03	26/12	09/02	30/10	15/09	23/02	10/11	13/04	22/04	01/12	05/01		01/09	11/08	13/10
Spennymoor Town	18/08	23/03	11/08	13/10	01/01	22/12	13/04	09/02	26/01	22/04	27/10	07/08	27/08	09/03	30/03	01/12	23/02	15/09	12/01		10/11	30/10
Stockport County	16/02	25/08	26/12	16/03	13/04	08/09	17/11	05/01	08/12	30/10	22/04	30/03	04/08	14/08	13/10	29/12	01/09	27/10	02/02	02/03		19/01
York City	27/04	11/08	09/03	09/02	27/08	23/03	22/12	03/11	20/10	26/01	18/08	01/01	01/12	29/09	12/01	15/09	10/11	23/02	06/04	20/04	07/08	

Please note that the above fixtures may be subject to change.

National League South Fixtures 2018/2019	Bath City	Billericay Town	Chelmsford City	Chippenham Town	Concord Rangers	Dartford	Dulwich Hamlet	Eastbourne Borough	East Thurrock United	Gloucester City	Hampton & Richmond Boro	Hemel Hempstead Town	Hungerford Town	Oxford City	Slough Town	St. Albans City	Torquay United	Truro City	Wealdstone	Welling United	Weston-super-Mare	Woking
Bath City		20/10	22/12	01/01	08/12	04/08	18/08	12/01	17/11	14/08	02/02	03/11	08/09	22/04	23/02	13/04	19/01	02/03	16/03	29/09	27/08	30/03
Billericay Town	27/04		01/01	12/01	07/08	15/09	27/10	30/10	16/02	13/10	06/04	20/04	23/03	01/12	10/11	27/08	09/03	09/02	11/08	26/01	18/08	22/12
Chelmsford City	25/08	26/12		20/10	02/03	19/01	13/08	16/02	03/11	01/12	05/01	29/12	02/02	30/03	01/09	29/09	04/08	17/11	22/04	08/09	16/03	13/04
Chippenham Town	26/12	25/08	27/04		01/09	13/10	06/04	27/10	05/01	15/09	29/12	09/02	16/02	02/03	07/08	16/03	20/04	26/01	17/11	11/08	01/12	03/11
Concord Rangers	16/02	19/01	30/10	22/12		14/08	02/02	01/01	20/10	04/08	10/11	01/12	18/08	13/04	09/03	22/04	23/03	29/09	12/01	27/08	30/03	08/09
Dartford	09/02	22/04	07/08	13/04	26/01		30/10	27/08	08/09	09/03	23/03	11/08	22/12	20/10	08/12	12/01	10/11	30/03	18/08	01/01	29/09	23/02
Dulwich Hamlet	05/01	30/03	26/01	29/09	11/08	02/03		08/08	26/12	25/08	01/09	16/02	13/04	17/11	29/12	03/11	01/12	16/03	08/09	09/02	20/10	22/04
Eastbourne Borough	01/09	02/03	08/12	30/03	26/12	29/12	19/01		14/08	05/01	23/02	17/11	20/10	16/03	25/08	08/09	02/02	03/11	29/09	22/04	13/04	04/08
East Thurrock Utd	23/03	08/12	09/03	18/08	27/04	20/04	01/01	26/01		06/04	30/10	27/10	10/11	09/02	15/09	22/12	13/10	11/08	23/02	07/08	12/01	27/08
Gloucester City	26/12	13/04	23/02	22/04	09/02	03/11	22/12	18/08	29/09		08/12	16/03	12/01	07/08	11/08	17/11	27/08	08/09	02/03	30/03	01/01	20/10
Hampton & Richmond	11/08	29/09	18/08	27/08	16/03	17/11	12/01	01/12	02/03	16/02		07/08	30/03	03/11	09/02	26/01	22/12	22/04	13/04	20/10	08/09	01/01
Hemel Hempstead T.	09/03	08/09	27/08	04/08	23/02	02/02	08/12	23/03	30/03	10/11	19/01		14/08	29/09	30/10	01/01	12/01	13/04	20/10	22/12	22/04	18/08
Hungerford Town	20/04	17/11	11/08	08/12	05/01	25/08	13/10	27/04	16/03	01/09	27/10	26/01		26/12	06/04	09/02	15/09	29/12	07/08	23/02	03/11	02/03
Oxford City	15/09	23/02	27/10	30/10	13/10	27/04	23/03	10/11	04/08	19/01	09/03	06/04	01/01		20/04	18/08	14/08	08/12	27/08	12/01	22/12	02/02
Slough Town	01/12	16/03	12/01	19/01	03/11	16/02	27/08	22/12	22/04	02/02	04/08	02/03	29/09	08/09		30/03	18/08	20/10	01/01	13/04	14/08	17/11
St. Albans City	13/10	29/12	06/04	10/11	15/09	01/09	09/03	20/04	25/08	23/03	14/08	26/12	04/08	05/01	27/10		27/04	23/02	08/12	30/10	02/02	19/01
Torquay United	07/08	03/11	09/02	08/09	17/11	16/03	23/02	11/08	13/04	29/12	25/08	01/09	22/04	26/01	05/01	20/10		26/12	30/03	08/12	02/03	29/09
Truro City	30/10	04/08	23/03	14/08	06/04	27/10	10/11	09/03	02/02	20/04	15/09	13/10	27/08	16/02	27/04	01/12	01/01		22/12	18/08	19/01	12/01
Wealdstone	10/11	02/02	15/09	23/03	25/08	05/01	20/04	06/04	01/12	29/10	13/10	27/04	19/01	29/12	26/12	16/02	27/10	01/09		09/03	04/08	13/08
Welling United	06/04	14/08	20/04	02/02	29/12	26/12	04/08	15/09	19/01	27/10	27/04	25/08	01/12	01/09	13/10	02/03	16/02	05/01	03/11		17/11	16/03
Weston-super-Mare	29/12	05/01	10/11	23/02	27/10	06/04	27/04	13/10	01/09	26/12	20/04	15/09	09/03	25/08	26/01	11/08	30/10	07/08	09/02	23/03		08/12
Woking	27/10	01/09	13/10	09/03	20/04	01/12	15/09	09/02	29/12	27/04	26/12	05/01	30/10	11/08	23/03	07/08	06/04	25/08	26/01	10/11	16/02	

Please note that the above fixtures may be subject to change.

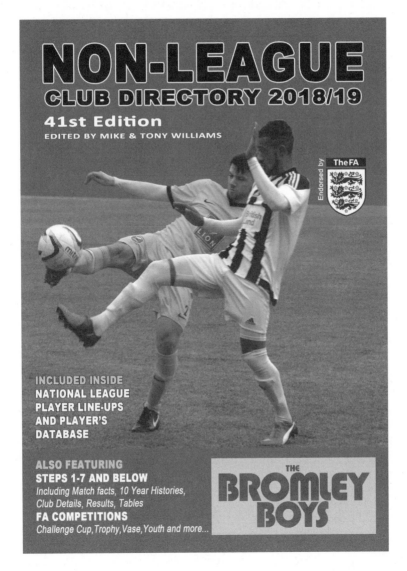

NON-LEAGUE
CLUB DIRECTORY 2018/19
41st Edition
EDITED BY MIKE & TONY WILLIAMS

Endorsed by The FA

**INCLUDED INSIDE
NATIONAL LEAGUE
PLAYER LINE-UPS
AND PLAYER'S
DATABASE**

**ALSO FEATURING
STEPS 1-7 AND BELOW**
*Including Match facts, 10 Year Histories,
Club Details, Results, Tables*
FA COMPETITIONS
Challenge Cup, Trophy, Vase, Youth and more...

THE
**BROMLEY
BOYS**

Now in its 41st year of publication, The Directory has developed into a comprehensive record of competitions within the non-league game and gives this level of football the publicity and prestige it deserves.

The Football Association has encouraged the development of the publication since its introduction as a small pocket book in 1978 and all their competitions such as The Cup, Trophy and Vase plus their Youth and Women's cups are featured.

Individual club pages highlight the top twelve divisions with club details, records and statistics plus senior players are featured in team photographs and within many action shots from league and cup football.

Major competitions within the nation's pyramid of domestic leagues are featured from levels 1-7 with many leagues outside of the top seven steps also featured.

Supporters' Guides and Tables books

Our Supporters' Guide series has been published since 1982 and the new 2019 editions contain the 2017/2018 Season's results and tables, Directions, Photographs, Telephone numbers, Parking information, Admission details, Disabled information and much more.

Our Football Tables books are perfect companions to the Supporters' Guides and contain historical Football League, Non-League and Scottish final tables up to the end of the 2018/2019 season.

THE SUPPORTERS' GUIDE TO PREMIER & FOOTBALL LEAGUE CLUBS 2019

This 35th edition covers all 92 Premiership and Football League clubs.   *Price £9.99*

NON-LEAGUE SUPPORTERS' GUIDE AND YEARBOOK 2019

This 27th edition covers all 68 clubs in Step 1 & Step 2 of Non-League football – the Vanarama National League, National League North and National League South.   *Price £9.99*

SCOTTISH FOOTBALL SUPPORTERS' GUIDE AND YEARBOOK 2019

The 26th edition featuring all Scottish Professional Football League, Highland League and Lowland League clubs.   *Price £9.99*

ENGLISH FOOTBALL LEAGUE & F.A. PREMIER LEAGUE TABLES 1888-2018

The 21st edition contains every Football League & F.A. Premier League final table plus play-off results and F.A. Cup and League Cup semi-final & final results.   *Price £9.99*

NON-LEAGUE FOOTBALL TABLES 1889-2018

The 16th edition contains final league tables for the 3 Leagues operating at Steps 3 and 4 of the pyramid, the Northern Premier League, Southern League and Isthmian League. This edition also contains tables for the Lancashire Alliance 1889-1935 plus historical notes about the Isthmian League and Northern Premier League.   *Price £9.99*

SCOTTISH FOOTBALL TABLES 1890-2018

The 8th edition contains final league tables for all Scottish Professional Football League, Scottish League, Scottish Premier League, Highland League and Lowland Football League seasons.   *Price £9.99*

These books are available UK & Surface post free from –

Soccer Books Limited (Dept. SBL)
72 St. Peter's Avenue
Cleethorpes, DN35 8HU
United Kingdom